I0411442

Congressional Research Service
Informing the legislative debate since 1914

Federal Student Loan Forgiveness and Loan Repayment Programs

Alexandra Hegji, Coordinator
Analyst in Social Policy

David P. Smole
Specialist in Education Policy

Elayne J. Heisler
Analyst in Health Services

July 22, 2014

Congressional Research Service

7-5700

www.crs.gov

R43571

Summary

Student loan forgiveness and loan repayment programs provide borrowers a means of having all or part of their student loan debt forgiven or repaid in exchange for work or service in specific fields or professions or following a prolonged period during which their student loan debt burden is high relative to their income. In both loan forgiveness and loan repayment programs, borrowers typically qualify for benefits by working or serving in certain capacities for a specified period of time or by satisfying other program requirements over an extended term. Upon qualifying for benefits, some or all of a borrower's student loan debt is forgiven or paid on his or her behalf.

One of the most important distinctions among these types of programs is whether the availability of benefits is incorporated into the loan terms and conditions and thus considered an entitlement to qualified borrowers, or whether benefits are made available to qualified borrowers at the discretion of the entity administering the program and subject to the availability of funds. For the purposes of this report, the former types of programs are referred to as *loan forgiveness* while the latter are referred to as *loan repayment*.

Loan forgiveness and loan repayment programs typically are intended to support one or more of the following goals:

- Provide a financial incentive to encourage individuals to enter public service.

- Provide a financial incentive to encourage individuals to enter a particular profession, occupation, or occupational specialty.

- Provide a financial incentive to encourage individuals to remain employed in a high-need profession or occupation—often in certain locations or at certain facilities.

- Provide debt relief to borrowers who, after repaying their student loans as a proportion of their income for an extended period of time, have not completely repaid their entire student loan debt.

The number and availability of loan forgiveness and loan repayment programs have expanded considerably since the establishment of the first major federal loan forgiveness program by the National Defense Education Act of 1958. Currently, over 50 loan forgiveness and loan repayment programs are authorized, and at least 30 of which were operational as of October 1, 2013.

While existing loan forgiveness and loan repayment programs may support similar broader goals, there is great variety across programs in their design and scope. For instance, some programs are widely available to all borrowers who meet program eligibility criteria. However, many programs are narrowly focused on supporting specific public service or workforce needs and are available only to individuals serving in certain occupations or working in certain geographic regions, or individuals employed by certain federal agencies. In some programs, the availability of benefits is incorporated into the terms and conditions of borrowers' loans and is more certain, whereas in other programs, the availability of benefits is subject to discretionary funding and award criteria. Programs are also distinguished by types of loans that qualify for forgiveness or repayment, qualifying periods of service, the amount of debt that may be discharged, and the tax treatment of discharged indebtedness.

Congress may explore whether loan forgiveness and loan repayment programs are effectively achieving policy objectives. Several issues might be examined. For instance, should multiple loan forgiveness and loan repayment programs continue to exist for providing debt relief to borrowers who engage in similar types of activities? Does the structure of some programs lead to a financial windfall for borrowers who engage in the same type of activity they might otherwise have in the absence of loan forgiveness and loan repayment benefits? Are programs appropriately targeted? Is sufficient information available to assess whether existing programs are effectively achieving their intended purposes?

Contents

Background and History of Loan Forgiveness and Loan Repayment Programs 1
    Early Student Loan Forgiveness and Repayment Programs 2
Overview of Federal Loan Forgiveness and Loan Repayment Programs 3
    Distinction among Loan Forgiveness and Loan Repayment Programs 3
    Loans Eligible for Forgiveness or Repayment 5
        HEA Federal Student Loan Programs 6
        Health Resources and Services Administration Loan Programs 9
        Private Education Loans 11
Loan Forgiveness and Loan Repayment Program Components 11
    Availability of Loan Forgiveness for Public Service Employment 12
    Availability of Loan Forgiveness Following Income-Dependent Repayment 13
    Availability of Loan Repayment for Public Service Employment 14
        Loan Repayment Programs Addressing Broad Employment Needs or Shortages 14
        Loan Repayment Programs to Recruit and Retain Federal
            Government Employees 17
    Borrower's Economic Circumstances 21
    Amount and Timing of Benefits 21
    Exclusions and Limitations 22
        Prohibition of Double Benefits 22
        Citizenship and Immigration Status 22
        Defaulted Loans 23
        Clawback Provisions 23
    Tax Treatment of Loan Forgiveness and Repayment Benefits 24
Effectiveness of Loan Forgiveness and Loan Repayment Programs 25
    Evidence of Effectiveness or Ineffectiveness 25
Cost of Loan Forgiveness and Loan Repayment Programs 28
    Loan Subsidy Costs 28
    Appropriated Program Costs 30
    Administrative Costs 30
    Estimated and Actual Costs for Loan Forgiveness and Loan Repayment Programs 31
        Cost Estimates for Selected Loan Forgiveness Programs 31
Issues for Congress 32
    Overlapping of Benefits Across Programs 32
    Debt Relief or Windfall? 33
    Data on Program Outcomes and Effectiveness 34
    Qualifying Loan Types and Amounts 35
    Variability of Selection Criteria Among Administering Agencies 35

Tables

Table 1. Loan Forgiveness for Public Service Employment Programs 12
Table 2. Loan Forgiveness Following Income-Dependent Repayment Programs 13

Table 3. Loan Repayment for Public Service Employment Programs Addressing Broad Employment Needs or Shortages... 15

Table 4. Loan Repayment for Public Service Employment in the Federal Government 17

Table B-1. Acronyms used in Table B-2 through Table B-6 124

Table B-2. Federal Student Loan Repayment and Forgiveness Programs 126

Table B-3. Federal Student Loan Repayment and Forgiveness Programs 131

Table B-4. Federal Student Loan Repayment and Forgiveness Programs 133

Table B-5. Federal Student Loan Repayment and Forgiveness Programs 136

Table B-6. Federal Student Loan Repayment and Forgiveness Programs 137

Appendixes

Appendix A. Program-Specific Details 37

Appendix B. Programs by Eligibility 124

Contacts

Author Contact Information... 140

Acknowledgements... 140

Background and History of Loan Forgiveness and Loan Repayment Programs

Federal student loan programs that make available loan forgiveness or repayment in return for service in certain professions or occupations have existed since the enactment of the National Defense Education Act of 1958 (NDEA; P.L. 85-864), which authorized the National Defense Student Loan (NDSL) program. In recognition of the high costs to individuals of borrowing to finance postsecondary education expenses and to address identified needs for individuals to perform certain types of service or work in certain occupations, an array of student loan forgiveness and repayment programs have been enacted. These programs offer borrowers a means to have all or part of their student loan debt forgiven or repaid in return for work or service in specific fields or professions or for satisfying certain conditions relating to borrower debt and income. Throughout the years, various federal loan forgiveness and loan repayment programs have been created, and presently, over 50 such programs exist, approximately 30 of which were operational as of October 1, 2013.

Loan forgiveness (sometimes also referred to as cancellation or discharge) programs and loan repayment programs are characterized by the federal government's forgiving, canceling, or discharging all or a portion of an individual's total student loan indebtedness or making loan payments on a borrower's behalf, upon the individual satisfying certain requirements. Loan forgiveness and loan repayment benefits are often contingent upon a borrower completing a period of employment in public service or in certain other occupations. Increasingly, however, loan forgiveness benefits have begun to be offered as a component of certain income-dependent student loan repayment plans. While the various programs operate somewhat differently, they are generally intended to support at least one of the following goals:

- Provide a financial incentive to encourage individuals to enter public service.

- Provide a financial incentive to encourage individuals to enter a particular profession, occupation, or occupational specialty.

- Provide a financial incentive to encourage individuals to remain employed in a high-need profession or occupation—often in certain locations or at certain facilities.

- Provide debt relief to borrowers who, after repaying their student loans as a proportion of their income for an extended period of time, have not completely repaid their entire student loan debt.

These types of loan forgiveness and loan repayment benefits provide debt relief to borrowers of federal student loans who make an active choice to enter public service or obtain employment in particular professions, occupations, or specialties, or to repay their loans according to an income-dependent repayment plan. Other forms of debt relief also may be available to borrowers who experience certain unfortunate circumstances. These forms of debt relief—which are beyond the scope of this report—include loan discharge for borrowers who become totally and permanently disabled, loan discharge upon death of the individual on whose behalf a loan was made, discharge for closure of the borrower's school, discharge for false certification of student eligibility, discharge for loans made without the borrower's authorization, discharge for unpaid refunds by a school following the borrower's withdrawal from school, and discharge in bankruptcy.[1]

Early Student Loan Forgiveness and Repayment Programs

One of the earliest federal student loan programs that made loan forgiveness available to borrowers was the NDSL program, authorized under the NDEA in 1958. The NDSL program was established, in part, as a response to the Union of Soviet Socialist Republics' 1957 launch of the Sputnik satellite.[2] Many members of Congress viewed this as an issue of national security, as they believed this event illustrated that the United States was falling behind in technological developments.

To address this perceived national security issue, Congress decided to target and fund improvements in education programs because national security required "the fullest development of mental resources and technical skills of its young men and women."[3] The establishment of the NDSL program made low-interest loans available to college students to help them pursue their studies. Also as part of the NDSL program, Congress authorized a student loan forgiveness component, which was intended to increase the number and quality of teachers in U.S. schools.[4] Specifically, students who taught full-time in a public elementary or secondary school were eligible to have up to half of their student loans cancelled.[5]

Over the years, the NDSL loan forgiveness provisions were amended, with the teacher loan forgiveness benefits targeted at individuals who were either teaching in elementary or secondary schools at which low-income students made up more than 30% of the enrollment or were teaching students with disabilities full-time. Loan forgiveness benefits were also expanded to be available to individuals serving in a Head Start program and those serving in an area of hostility while in the armed forces. Through these provisions, qualified borrowers became eligible to have a portion of their loans canceled based on the number of years of public service completed.[6] The NDSL program was incorporated into the Higher Education Act of 1965 (HEA; P.L. 89-329) through the Education Amendments of 1972 (P.L. 92-318); and was later renamed the Federal Perkins Loan Program[7] by amendments made through the Higher Education Amendments of 1986 (P.L. 99-498).

---

[1] For additional information on these forms of debt relief, see U.S. Department of Education, Federal Student Aid, "Repay Your Loans: Forgiveness, Cancellation, and Discharge," https://studentaid.ed.gov/repay-loans/forgiveness-cancellation.

[2] C. Ronald Kimberling, "Federal Student Aid: A History and Critical Analysis," in *The Academy in Crisis: The Political Economy of Higher Education*, ed. John W. Sommer (Oakland: The Independent Institute, 1995), pp. 69-70.

[3] P.L. 85-864 §101.

[4] U.S. Congress, Senate Committee on Labor and Public Welfare, *National Defense Education Act of 1958*, Report to accompany S. 4237, 85th Cong., 2nd sess., August 8, 1958, Report No. 2242, p. 10.

[5] P.L. 85-864 §205(b)(3).

[6] For instance, individuals teaching students with disabilities full-time were eligible to have 100% of their loans forgiven, while individuals serving in the armed services in an area of hostility were eligible to have 50% of their loans forgiven. CRS Report CD832039, *The Experience with Loan Forgiveness and Service Payback in Federal and State Student Aid Programs*, by Jim Stedman; archived, available on request.

[7] For additional information on the Federal Perkins Loan program, see CRS Report RL31618, *Campus-Based Student Financial Aid Programs Under the Higher Education Act*, by Alexandra Hegji and David P. Smole.

Subsequent to the enactment of the NDEA, other federal student loan forgiveness and repayment programs were established to target borrowers who entered other professions and worked in high-need areas. For instance, in 1965, a loan forgiveness component modeled after the NDSL was incorporated into the Health Professions Student Loan Program (HPSLP), authorized under the Public Health Service Act (PHSA; P.L. 89-290). Under this program, borrowers who practiced medicine in locations with a health manpower shortage (as defined) could have up to 50% of their loans forgiven.[8] Following these early student loan repayment and forgiveness programs, many additional programs were enacted and currently over 50 such programs exist.

Overview of Federal Loan Forgiveness and Loan Repayment Programs

This report identifies and describes federal student loan forgiveness and loan repayment programs that are currently authorized by federal law. It provides brief, summary descriptions of identified programs. These program descriptions are intended to provide policy makers with general information about the purpose of existing programs and how they are designed to operate. The program descriptions are not intended to be comprehensive in nature. Readers interested in comprehensive details about a particular program are encouraged to refer to additional resources, including federal statutes, regulations, and agency guidance. Citations are provided for the various programs identified in this report.

Over 50 federal student loan forgiveness and repayment programs are currently authorized under federal law. Although each program is designed to operate somewhat differently, they are all intended to provide debt relief to borrowers who perform specified types of service, enter into and remain employed in certain professions, serve in certain locations, or repay their loans according to an income-dependent repayment plan for an extended period of time.

Each of the various programs has unique characteristics and may be distinguished by features such as differing borrower eligibility criteria, benefit amounts, the means through which benefits are provided, or how the program is funded. In this overview, several parameters are identified and used to broadly characterize various aspects of the currently authorized programs. As some of the terms commonly used to identify the benefits offered through these programs (e.g., loan forgiveness, cancellation, or repayment) are often used inconsistently from program to program, this report's use of a consistent set of parameters to characterize various aspects of the programs facilitates the description and examination of some of the similarities and differences between the various programs.

Distinction among Loan Forgiveness and Loan Repayment Programs

In employment-focused loan forgiveness and loan repayment programs, a borrower typically must work or serve in a certain function, profession, or geographic location for a specified period of time to qualify for benefits. In repayment plan-based loan forgiveness programs, a borrower

---

[8] CRS Report LB2301, *The Experience with Loan Forgiveness and Service Payback in Federal and State Student Aid Programs*, by Jim Stedman; archived, available on request.

typically must repay according to an income-dependent repayment plan for a specified period of time to qualify for benefits. At the end of the specified term, some or all of the individual's qualifying student loan debt is forgiven or paid on his or her behalf. The individual is thus relieved of responsibility for paying that portion of his or her student loan debt. One of the most important distinctions among these types of programs is whether the availability of benefits is incorporated into the loan terms and conditions and is thus considered an entitlement to qualified borrowers or whether benefits are made available to qualified borrowers at the discretion of the entity administering the program and whether the benefits are subject to the availability of funds. For the purposes of this report, the former types of programs are referred to as *loan forgiveness* while the latter are referred to as *loan repayment*.

In general, loan forgiveness benefits are broadly available to borrowers of qualified loans. The availability of these benefits is expressed to borrowers in their loan documents, such as the master promissory note and the borrower's rights and responsibilities statement.[9] A borrower who satisfies the loan forgiveness program's eligibility criteria, as set forth in the loan terms and conditions, is entitled to the loan forgiveness benefits. Benefits that are entitlements to qualified borrowers are generally funded through mandatory appropriations and accounted for as part of federal student loan subsidy costs, which are discussed in detail later in the section titled "Cost of Loan Forgiveness and Loan Repayment Programs." There are two broad categories of loan forgiveness benefits: loan forgiveness for public service employment and loan forgiveness following income-dependent repayment.

Loan repayment programs also provide debt relief to borrowers for service in a specific function, profession, or location. However, in contrast to employment-focused loan forgiveness programs, the entity that administers a loan repayment program typically either directly repays some or all of the qualified borrower's student loan debt on his or her behalf or provides funding to a separate entity for purposes of implementing a loan repayment program and making such payments. Loan repayment benefits are generally offered through programs that are separate or distinct from the program through which a federal student loan is made. In many instances, these programs are designed to address broad employment needs or shortages (e.g., within a specific occupation or geographic location), while other such programs are intended to help individual federal agencies recruit and retain qualified employees, often serving as an additional form of compensation to targeted employees, who may be harder to recruit or retain. Both types of loan repayment benefits are generally available to a limited number of qualified borrowers. Typically, loan repayment benefits are discretionary and their availability is subject to the appropriation of funds.

The text box below provides a summary of some of the distinguishing features of the three categories of debt relief programs examined in this report: programs that provide loan forgiveness for public service employment, programs that provide loan forgiveness following income-dependent repayment, and programs that provide loan repayment for public service employment.

---

[9] Some loan forgiveness programs have been established and made available to individuals who have already borrowed their loans. The resulting change to the terms and conditions of an existing loan program is referred to as a loan modification.

Distinguishing Features of Loan Forgiveness and Loan Repayment Programs

Loan forgiveness for public service employment

- Provides debt relief for borrowers employed in specific occupations, for specific employers, or in public service

- Benefits are potentially available to an open-ended number of qualified borrowers

- Availability of benefits is generally incorporated into the terms and conditions of certain federal student loans

- Benefits are considered an entitlement to qualified borrowers

- Funding for benefits is typically incorporated into loan subsidy costs

Loan forgiveness following income-dependent repayment

- Provides debt relief for borrowers who, after repaying their student loans as a proportion of their income for an extended period of time, have not repaid their entire student loan debt

- Benefits are potentially available to an open-ended number of qualified borrowers

- Availability of benefits are generally incorporated into the terms and conditions of certain federal student loans

- Benefits are considered an entitlement to qualified borrowers

- Funding for benefits are typically incorporated into loan subsidy costs

Loan repayment for public service employment

- Provides debt relief for borrowers employed in specific occupations, for specific employers, or in public service

- Benefits are generally available to a limited number of qualified borrowers, subject to the appropriation of funds

- Program-specific benefits may be designed to address broad employment needs or shortages in a specific occupation or geographic location, or may be offered by government agencies to support the recruitment and retention of qualified employees

- Benefits are not considered an entitlement to qualified borrowers

- Funding for benefits is typically provided through discretionary appropriations

Loans Eligible for Forgiveness or Repayment

There are three broad categories of loans that may be eligible for inclusion in federal loan forgiveness and loan repayment programs:

1. Federal student loans made through programs authorized by Title IV of the Higher Education Act (HEA) and administered by the U.S. Department of Education (ED), Office of Federal Student Aid (FSA).

2. Student loans made through programs authorized by Title VII and Title VIII of the Public Health Service Act (PHSA) and administered by the U.S. Department of Health and Human Services (HHS), Health Resources and Services Administration (HRSA).

3. Private (nonfederal) education loans.

For most federal loan forgiveness and loan repayment programs, eligible loans include only federal student loans made through HEA or PHSA programs; however, for a small number of programs, eligible loans also include private education loans. Brief summaries of student loan types that may be eligible for loan forgiveness or loan repayment are provided below.

HEA Federal Student Loan Programs

Federal student loans are currently made through two HEA, Title IV federal student aid programs—the Direct Loan program and the Federal Perkins Loan program. Until June 30, 2010, federal student loans were also made through the Federal Family Education Loan (FFEL) program, a guaranteed loan program. FFEL program loans were made with terms and conditions that were similar to those of loans offered through the Direct Loan program.[10]

In the Direct Loan program, loans are made by the government with federal capital. ED administers the program, and activities such as loan origination, servicing, and collection are performed by federal contractors. In the FFEL program, loans were made by nonfederal lenders with nonfederal capital. These entities were responsible for originating, holding, and servicing these loans. Nonprofit guaranty agencies administer federal loan insurance and process loan forgiveness benefits. During the period when the FFEL and Direct Loan programs both operated, one set of loan types was made through the FFEL program and another similar set of loan types was made through the Direct Loan program. While these two sets of loan types had borrower terms and conditions that were quite similar, some of the ways in which they differed pertained to availability of loan forgiveness benefits. Where applicable, differences in the availability of loan forgiveness benefits are noted in the discussion that follows.[11]

In the Perkins Loan program, loans are made by institutions of higher education (IHEs) with a combination of capital provided by the federal government and capital provided by the institution. In the Perkins Loan program, the institution serves as the lender and is responsible for originating and servicing Perkins Loans and for processing loan cancelation benefits.[12]

The following loan types comprise the primary types of loans that are currently being made—or in recent years have been made—through HEA, Title IV federal student loan programs.

Subsidized Loans

In the Direct Loan program, Direct Subsidized Loans are available only to undergraduate students who demonstrate financial need.[13] The federal government "subsidizes" these loans by not assessing interest charges while the borrower is enrolled in an eligible academic program on at least a half-time basis, during a six-month grace period prior the loan entering repayment status,[14]

---

[10] The authority to make new loans through the FFEL program was terminated by the SAFRA Act, part of the Health Care and Education Reconciliation Act of 2010 (HCERA; P.L. 111-152). For additional information on the SAFRA Act, see CRS Report R41127, *The SAFRA Act: Education Programs in the FY2010 Budget Reconciliation*, coordinated by Cassandria Dortch.

[11] For detailed information on the loan types made through the Direct Loan and FFEL programs, see CRS Report R40122, *Federal Student Loans Made Under the Federal Family Education Loan Program and the William D. Ford Federal Direct Loan Program: Terms and Conditions for Borrowers*, by David P. Smole.

[12] For additional information on the Federal Perkins Loan program, see CRS Report RL31618, *Campus-Based Student Financial Aid Programs Under the Higher Education Act*, by Alexandra Hegji and David P. Smole.

[13] Prior to July 1, 2010, loans with substantially similar terms and conditions as Direct Subsidized Loans—Subsidized Stafford Loans—were made through the FFEL program. For the remainder of this report, Direct Subsidized Loans and FFEL Subsidized Stafford Loans are referred to jointly as *Subsidized Loans*; however, in instances where loan forgiveness or loan repayment benefits are only available to borrowers of one loan type, this distinction is noted.

[14] The interest subsidy during the six-month grace period does not apply to Direct Subsidized Loans for which the first disbursement was made from July 1, 2012 through June 30, 2014.

and during periods of authorized deferment. Prior to July 1, 2012, Direct Subsidized Loans were also available to graduate and professional students.[15] Borrowing limits restrict the amounts that students may borrow during a given academic year and in the aggregate over multiple years. In FY2013, 8.5 million Direct Subsidized Loans, totaling $27.4 billion were made.[16]

Unsubsidized Loans

Direct Unsubsidized Loans are available to undergraduate, graduate, and professional students. Students are not required to demonstrate financial need to be eligible to borrow these loans.[17] As a non-need-based loan, loan proceeds may be used to finance portions of a student's cost of attendance (COA) that would otherwise be expected to be met by the student's expected family contribution (EFC) toward postsecondary education expenses. For these loans, the borrower is responsible for paying all the interest that accrues on the loan from the time it is disbursed, although interest payments may be deferred until the loan enters repayment status. Unsubsidized Loan borrowing is also limited by annual and aggregate borrowing limits. In FY2013, 8.5 million Direct Unsubsidized Loans, totaling $29.0 billion were made.[18]

PLUS Loans

Direct PLUS Loans are available to the parents of undergraduate students who are dependent on them for financial support, as well as to graduate and professional students.[19] Like Unsubsidized Loans, these are non-need-based loans and may be used to finance postsecondary education expenses that would otherwise be expected to be met by a student's EFC. There are no explicit limits to the amount an individual may borrow in PLUS Loans. Rather, each year, an individual may borrow up to the amount that the COA of the student on whose behalf the loan is made is greater than his or her estimated financial assistance (EFA) from other sources (e.g., Pell Grants, Subsidized Loans, Unsubsidized Loans, private scholarships, etc.). In FY2013, 0.8 million Direct PLUS Loans, totaling $10.3 billion, were made to parents of undergraduate students and 0.5 million Direct PLUS Loans, totaling $7.7 billion, were made to graduate and professional students.[20]

---

[15] The authority to make Subsidized Loans to graduate and professional students was eliminated under the Budget Control Act of 2011 (BCA; P.L. 112-25). For additional information on changes made to the Direct Loan program by the BCA, see CRS Report R41965, *The Budget Control Act of 2011*, by Bill Heniff Jr., Elizabeth Rybicki, and Shannon M. Mahan.

[16] U.S. Department of Education, FY 2015 Department of Education Justifications of Appropriation Estimates to the Congress, Volume II, Student Loans Overview, p. S-20.

[17] Prior to July 1, 2010, loans with substantially similar terms and conditions—Unsubsidized Stafford Loans—were made through the FFEL program. For the remainder of this report, Direct Unsubsidized Loans and FFEL Unsubsidized Stafford Loans are referred to jointly as Unsubsidized Loans; however, in instances where loan forgiveness or loan repayment benefits are only available to borrowers of one loan type, this distinction is noted.

[18] U.S. Department of Education, *FY 2015 Department of Education Justifications of Appropriation Estimates to the Congress*, Volume II, Student Loans Overview, p. S-20.

[19] When first established, PLUS Loans were referred to as Parent Loans for Undergraduate Students. Prior to July 1, 2010, PLUS Loans were made through the FFEL program with terms and conditions that were mostly similar to Direct PLUS Loans. For the remainder of this report, Direct PLUS Loans and FFEL PLUS Loans are referred to jointly as *PLUS Loans*; however, in instances where loan forgiveness or loan repayment benefits are only available to borrowers of one loan type, this distinction is noted.

[20] U.S. Department of Education, *FY 2015 Department of Education Justifications of Appropriation Estimates to the Congress*, Volume II, Student Loans Overview, p. S-20.

Consolidation Loans

Direct Consolidation Loans allow borrowers with existing federal student loans to combine their loan obligations into a single loan and to extend their repayment period.

Consolidation Loans must include at least one loan made through either the Direct Loan or the FFEL program. In addition, Consolidation Loans may include loans made through the federal student loan programs authorized or previously authorized under Title IV of the HEA[21] and loans made through the following programs authorized under Title VII and Title VIII of the PHSA (described below):

- Health Professions Student Loans (HPSL)
- Loans for Disadvantaged Students (LDS)
- Nursing Student Loans (NSL)
- Health Education Assistance Loans (HEAL)

That borrowers may incorporate different loan types into a Consolidation Loan is particularly relevant in the examination of loan forgiveness and loan repayment programs. This characteristic of Consolidation Loans facilitates the extension of certain loan forgiveness and loan repayment benefits to borrowers of loans originally made without those benefits upon such loans being incorporated into a Consolidation Loan.

The Direct Consolidation Loans currently being made are fixed rate loans for which the interest rate is based on the weighted average interest rate of the loans being consolidated, rounded up to the nearest higher one-eighth of 1%.[22] In FY2013, 0.7 million Direct Consolidation Loans, totaling $27.5 billion, were made.[23]

Perkins Loans

Perkins Loans are available to undergraduate and graduate and professional students. Perkins Loans must be made reasonably available to all eligible students, with priority given to students with exceptional financial need. Interest on Perkins Loans is fixed at 5% per year, and interest does not accrue prior to a borrower's beginning repayment nor during periods of authorized deferment. Borrowers who are engaged in certain types of public service may have a portion of

---

[21] These loan types (some of which are no longer being disbursed) are Federal Perkins Loans, Guaranteed Student Loans, Federal Insured Student Loans (FISL), National Direct Student Loans, National Defense Student Loans, Supplemental Loans for Students (SLS), and Auxiliary Loans to Assist Students (ALAS).

[22] Prior to July 1, 2010, Consolidation Loans were made through both the Direct Loan and FFEL programs. The terms and conditions applicable to a Consolidation Loan depend on when the loan was made. Prior to July 1, 2006, there were notable differences between the terms and conditions of Direct Consolidation Loans and those of FFEL Consolidation Loans. However, for loans made after July 1, 2006, the terms and conditions of loans made under both programs are substantially similar. For the remainder of this report, Direct Consolidation Loans and FFEL Consolidation Loans are referred to jointly as *Consolidation Loans*; however, in instances where loan forgiveness or loan repayment benefits are only available to borrowers of one loan type, this distinction is noted.

[23] U.S. Department of Education, *FY 2015 Department of Education Justifications of Appropriation Estimates to the Congress*, Volume II, Student Loans Overview, p. S-20.

---

their Perkins Loans cancelled for each complete year of service. In FY2013, 0.5 million Perkins Loans, totaling $1.0 billion, were made.[24]

Health Resources and Services Administration Loan Programs

HRSA, within HHS, makes student loans to specific health professions students through five loan programs authorized under Title VII and Title VIII of the PHSA. Collectively these programs made 19,530 loans in academic year 2012-2013 for a total of $131 million.[25] The five programs are described below.[26]

Health Professions Student Loans

This program provides low interest rate loans to full-time students who are pursuing degrees in dentistry, optometry, pharmacy, podiatric medicine, or veterinary medicine. The program is administered by schools that select participants who are citizens, nationals, or lawful permanent residents of the United States and financially needy.[27] For academic year 2012-2013, HRSA estimated that it made 7,546 loans, totaling $64 million.[28]

Primary Care Loans

This program provides 5% fixed interest rate loans to full-time students who are pursuing degrees in allopathic or osteopathic medicine. The program is administered by individual medical schools that select participants who are citizens, nationals, or lawful permanent residents of the United States and financially needy. In exchange for receiving a primary care loan, students must complete a residency in a primary care field (family medicine, internal medicine, pediatrics, preventive medicine, osteopathic general practice or combined programs in internal medicine and pediatrics) and practice in a primary care field for 10 years. Loan recipients who fail to meet the service requirements must repay their primary care loans at a higher interest rate of 7%.[29] For academic year 2012-2013, HRSA estimated that it made 362 loans, totaling $23 million.[30]

---

[24] U.S. Department of Education, *FY 2015 Department of Education Justifications of Appropriation Estimates to the Congress*, Volume II, Student Financial Assistance, p. Q-42.

[25] Email Communication, Health Resources and Services Administration, Office of Legislation, May 6, 2014.

[26] For additional information on PHSA loans, see U.S. Department of Health and Human Services, Health Resources and Services Administration, "Loans & Scholarships," at http://www hrsa.gov/loanscholarships/index html; for information on the Nurse Faculty Loan Program, see U.S. Department of Health and Human Services, Health Resources and Services Administration, "Nurse Faculty Loan Program (NFLP)," at http://bhpr hrsa.gov/nursing/grants/ nflp.html.

[27] U.S. Department of Health and Human Services, Health Resources and Services Administration, "Health Professions Student Loans," at http://www hrsa.gov/loanscholarships/loans/healthprofessions html.

[28] Email Communication, Health Resources and Services Administration, Office of Legislation, May 6, 2014.

[29] U.S. Department of Health and Human Services, Health Resources and Services Administration, "Primary Care Loans," at http://www hrsa.gov/loanscholarships/loans/primarycare.html.

[30] Email Communication, Health Resources and Services Administration, Office of Legislation, May 6, 2014.

Loans for Disadvantaged Students

This program provides need-based, low interest rate loans to students from disadvantaged backgrounds—defined as coming from a background that has inhibited the individual from pursuing a health professional degree or coming from a low-income background based on the family's income—who are pursuing degrees in allopathic or osteopathic medicine, optometry, podiatry, pharmacy or veterinary medicine. The program is administered by individual schools that select students who are citizens, nationals, or lawful permanent residents of the United States.[31] For academic year 2012-2013, HRSA estimated that it made 1,262 loans, totaling $15 million.[32]

Nursing Student Loans

This program provides low interest rate loans to students who are pursuing studies that lead to a diploma, associate, baccalaureate, or graduate degree in nursing. The program is administered by nursing schools that select participants who are citizens, nationals, or lawful permanent residents of the United States and financially needy.[33] For academic year 2012-2013, HRSA estimated that it made 10,360 loans, totaling $29 million.[34]

Nurse Faculty Loans

This program provides loans to registered nurses who are completing their graduate studies necessary to become qualified nursing school faculty. The program is administered by individual nursing schools that offer eligible advanced masters or doctoral degree nursing programs. Nursing schools select participants for loans and may also offer loan forgiveness (see "Nursing Faculty Loan Repayment Program" in **Appendix A**.[35] In FY2012, Nursing Faculty Loans were made to 2,259 nursing students, totaling $27.5 million.[36]

Health Education Assistance Loans

A sixth program, Health Education Assistance Loans (HEALs), authorized in Title VII, Part A-I of the PHSA, no longer makes new loans, but the program continues to receive an appropriation to administer outstanding loans.[37] HEALs were gradually phased out between1995 and1999 but were available to students to support their pursuit of degrees in allopathic and osteopathic

---

[31] U.S. Department of Health and Human Services, Health Resources and Services Administration, "Loans for Disadvantaged Students," at http://www hrsa.gov/loanscholarships/loans/disadvantaged html.

[32] Email Communication, Health Resources and Services Administration, Office of Legislation, May 6, 2014.

[33] U.S. Department of Health and Human Services, Health Resources and Services Administration, "Nursing Student Loans," at http://www hrsa.gov/loanscholarships/loans/nursing html.

[34] Email Communication, Health Resources and Services Administration, Office of Legislation, May 6, 2014.

[35] U.S. Department of Health and Human Services, Health Resources and Services Administration, "Nurse Faculty Loan Program (NFLP)," At http://bhpr hrsa.gov/nursing/grants/nflp html.

[36] U.S. Department of Health and Human Services, *FY2015 Health Resources and Services Administration Justification of Estimates for Appropriations Committees*, p. 186 and Email communication, Health Resources and Services Administration, Office of Legislation, May 6, 2014.

[37] Authority for the administration of the HEAL program was transferred to the Department of Education under the Consolidated Appropriations Act, 2014 (P.L. 113-76).

medicine, dentistry, veterinary medicine, optometry, podiatry, public health, pharmacy, chiropractic, and graduate programs in health administration, clinical psychology, and allied health professions. Although the authority to make new HEALs has been terminated, borrowers of HEALs remain responsible for making payments on their loans.

Private Education Loans

In addition to the student loans made through the federal student loan programs identified above, student loans are also made by a variety of nonfederal entities. The most common of these are student loans made by private financial institutions (e.g., banks, credit unions), student loans made through state-supported loan programs, and loans made by IHEs. These types of loans are sometimes referred to as private student loans or alternative loans. The terms and conditions of private education loans are specified by the entity responsible for making these loans. While private education loans are not made through federal loan programs, a small number of federal loan repayment programs make benefits available to borrowers of some types of these loans.

Loan Forgiveness and Loan Repayment Program Components

All student loan forgiveness and loan repayment programs provide some form of debt relief to borrowers who satisfy certain eligibility criteria. While these programs all support the broad common purpose of providing borrowers with debt relief, they are distinguished by unique program characteristics and features. This section of the report first outlines the three categories of debt relief programs discussed above (see "Distinction among Loan Repayment and Loan Forgiveness") and the qualifying criteria for borrowers associated with these three broad categories. It then identifies a number of program components or parameters that are used to characterize or classify the various programs and to facilitate the examination of and comparison between the various programs using a common terminology. Major program components examined include types of qualifying service, the consideration of borrower economic circumstances, amounts and timing of debt relief, and exclusions or limitations on benefits. For program-specific details on any of the programs discussed in this section, see **Appendix A**.

This section presents the primary categories of debt relief programs largely in order of their potential scope of availability to borrowers. First, the loan forgiveness entitlement programs are presented, as they are potentially the largest in scale, with programs providing loan forgiveness for public service presented first and then programs providing loan forgiveness as a component of income-dependent repayment plans.[38] Programs providing loan repayment for broad public service or employment needs are then presented, because their availability to borrowers is generally limited to a discrete number of individuals and they are smaller in scale than programs providing loan forgiveness. Finally, programs providing loan repayment for public service in government employment are presented, as they are generally more narrowly targeted to meet

---

[38] Programs providing loan forgiveness following income-dependent repayment have the potential to be larger in scale than programs providing loan forgiveness for public service because their availability is not contingent on an individual's completion of a specific service requirement. They are presented second in this discussion, as their availability has only recently expanded as a new variation of federal loan forgiveness benefits that traditionally were available only after an individual's completion of specified types of public service.

agency-specific recruitment and retention needs and are likely the smallest in scale of the loan repayment and forgiveness programs.

Availability of Loan Forgiveness for Public Service Employment

As described above, loan forgiveness for public service employment provides debt relief to qualified borrowers employed in certain occupations, for specific employers, or in public service. These benefits are considered entitlements and are written into the terms and conditions of widely available federal student loans (e.g., Direct Loan Subsidized and Unsubsidized Loans and Perkins Loans). They are potentially available to an open-ended number of qualified borrowers.

Table 1 provides a summary of the various loan forgiveness for public service employment programs offered. It highlights whether forgiveness benefits are available to borrowers who are employed with a single specified employer, one of multiple eligible employers, or if there is no specific employer requirement. It also highlights whether benefits are available to borrowers who are employed in a single specified occupation, one of multiple eligible occupations; or if there is no specific occupation requirement. Finally, it highlights whether a borrower must qualify based, in part, on their economic circumstances during repayment. The table also provides details on the operational status of the program. Programs are listed in descending order intended to be reflective of scale of benefits made available to borrowers.

Table 1. Loan Forgiveness for Public Service Employment Programs

Program Requirements and Details

Program	Eligible Employer(s)	Eligible Occupations	Income-Dependent (Y/N)	Operational Notes
Direct Loan Public Service Loan Forgiveness	Multiple	Multiple	Y	Currently active[a]; benefits may be received no earlier than October 2017
Stafford Loan Forgiveness for Teachers	Multiple	Single	N	Currently active[a]
Federal Perkins Loan Cancellation	Multiple	Multiple	N	Currently active[a]

Source: CRS analysis of applicable statutory provisions in the Higher Education Act.

a. A program is considered to have been active if, since October 1, 2013, borrowers have been eligible to qualify for or begin qualifying for loan forgiveness benefits under the program.

Table 1 illustrates that although loan forgiveness benefits are entitlements that are potentially available to a wide array of borrowers, to qualify for benefits borrowers must still meet specific eligibility criteria, including completing a specific type of service or entering into a particular occupation or profession.

All three programs are widely available to individuals serving as teachers, while Federal Perkins Loan Cancellation is available to individuals who also serve in other specific public service occupations, such as law enforcement personnel and public defenders, and Direct Loan Public Service Loan Forgiveness is available to an even broader array of individuals who are employed full-time in public service, which includes employment in federal, state, local, or tribal government agencies, organizations and certain nonprofit organizations. However, unlike the other programs, its availability is also dependent on borrowers' economic circumstances during repayment.

Additionally, borrowers under these programs must serve for a minimum period of time. For these loan forgiveness programs, service commitments generally last between one year (for partial benefits) and ten years.

Availability of Loan Forgiveness Following Income-Dependent Repayment

Loan forgiveness following income-dependent repayment provides debt relief to borrowers who repay their federal student loans as a proportion of their income for an extended period of time but who have not repaid their entire student loan debt. These benefits are considered entitlements and are written into the terms and conditions of widely available federal student loans (e.g., Direct Subsidized Loans, Direct Unsubsidized Loans, and Perkins Loans). They are potentially available to an open-ended number of qualified borrowers. These programs are potentially available to a large number of borrowers; however, these programs are distinct from those that target public service employment.

Table 2 provides a summary of the various loan forgiveness programs that provide debt relief to individuals following income-dependent repayment. The table also provides details on the operational status of the program.

Although it is unclear how many individual borrowers may benefit from these programs, as forgiveness benefits have not yet been realized under any of them, the table is organized according to the scale of benefits that might be realized by borrowers at the culmination of income-dependent repayment. The Income-Contingent Repayment (ICR) Plan A (Pay As You Earn) offers the most generous benefits currently available to borrowers—debt relief after 20 years of repayment based on 10% of discretionary income. The Income-Based Repayment (IBR) Plan for New Borrowers on or after July 1, 2014, will offer essentially the same level of benefits to individuals who are new borrowers on or after July 1, 2014. The IBR Plan for pre-July 1, 2014, borrowers offers debt relief after 25 years of repayment based on 15% of discretionary income and has been available to borrowers since 2009. Debt relief following 25 years of repayment according to ICR Plan B has been available to borrowers since 1994.

Table 2. Loan Forgiveness Following Income-Dependent Repayment Programs

Program Requirements and Details

Program	Income-Dependent (Y/N)	Operational Notes
Income-Contingent Repayment Plan A (Pay As You Earn)	Y	Borrowers became eligible to repay under this plan on December 21, 2012

Income-Based Repayment Plan for New Borrowers on or after July 1, 2014	Y	Borrowers will become eligible to repay under this plan after July 1, 2014
Income-Based Repayment Plan for pre-July 1, 2014 Borrowers	Y	Borrowers became eligible to repay under this plan after July 1, 2009
Income-Contingent Repayment Plan B	Y	Borrowers became eligible to repay under this plan on July 1, 1994

Source: CRS analysis of relevant statutory and regulatory provisions.

Table 2 illustrates that the various programs that provide loan forgiveness following income-dependent repayment are widely available to a potentially open-ended number of borrowers who meet income-driven qualifications. Unlike loan forgiveness or repayment programs that seek to encourage borrowers to enter into certain service or occupational commitments, no such employer-specific or occupational or service requirements exist for these programs. Rather, under each of the above programs, borrowers generally must make monthly payments towards their qualifying federal student loans for a specified period of time (between 20 and 25 years). The amount of monthly payments is determined based on factors including the amount of the student loan debt, family size, and adjusted gross income; monthly payments are capped at a percentage of a borrower's discretionary income (between 10% and 20%) or other income-dependent criteria. At the end of each program's repayment period, the outstanding balance of a borrower's loans is then forgiven and they are no longer responsible for payments on their loans.

Availability of Loan Repayment for Public Service Employment

Loan repayment for public service employment provides debt relief benefits to borrowers employed in specific occupations, for specific employers, or in public service. Some of these program benefits are often used to meet broad employment needs or shortages (e.g., within specific occupations or geographic locations), while others are intended to help individual government agencies recruit and retain qualified employees and often serve as additional compensation, similar to benefits offered by private employers. Both types of loan repayment for public service employment are generally available to a limited number of qualified borrowers, subject to the appropriation of program funds; they are not considered entitlements to qualified borrowers.

Loan Repayment Programs Addressing Broad Employment Needs or Shortages

Loan repayment programs addressing broad employment needs or shortages are generally available to a limited number of qualified borrowers and subject to the appropriation of program funds. These programs are smaller in scale, when considering their availability to borrowers, than are the previously discussed loan forgiveness programs.

Table 3 provides a summary of the various loan repayment programs offered for the purposes of meeting broad employment needs or shortages. It highlights whether repayment benefits are available to borrowers who are employed with a single specified employer, one of multiple eligible employers, or if no particular employer is specified. It also highlights whether benefits are available to borrowers who are employed in a single specified occupation, one of multiple eligible occupations; or if there is no specific occupational requirement. Finally, it highlights whether borrowers must qualify based, in part, on their economic circumstances.

The table is organized by operational status of each program, and within each operational subheading, programs are grouped by administering department or agency. Unlike the loan forgiveness programs presented above, these programs are not grouped by the potential scope of availability to borrowers and financial resources used to provide benefits, because such data are inconsistently available across programs.

Table 3. Loan Repayment for Public Service Employment Programs Addressing Broad Employment Needs or Shortages

Program Requirements and Details

Program	Eligible Employers(s)	Eligible Occupation(s)	Income-Dependent (Y/N)
Currently Active Programs[a]			
Veterinary Medication LRP	Multiple	Single	N
Indian Health Service LRP	Multiple	Single	N
National Health Service Corps LRP	Multiple	Single	N
National Health Service Corps Students to Service LRP	Multiple	Single	N
National Health Service Corps State LRP	Multiple	Single	N
National Institutes of Health Extramural LRP: Health Disparities Research	Multiple	Single	N
National Institutes of Health Extramural LRP: Contraception and Infertility Research	Multiple	Single	N
National Institutes of Health Extramural LRP: Clinical Research	Multiple	Single	N
National Institutes of Health Extramural LRP: Pediatric Research	Multiple	Single	N
Loan Repayments for Health Professional School Faculty	Multiple	Single	N
General, Pediatric, and Public Health Dentistry Faculty Loan Repayment	Multiple	Single	N
Nursing Education LRP (NURSE Corps)	Multiple	Single	N
Nurse Faculty LRP	Multiple	Single	N
John R. Justice Loan Repayment for Prosecutors and Public Defenders	Multiple	Single	N

Program	Eligible Employers(s)	Eligible Occupation(s)	Income-Dependent (Y/N)
Previously Active Programs			
Civil Legal Assistance Attorney LRP[b]	Multiple	Single	N
Public Health Workforce LRP[b]	Multiple	Single	N
Never Active Programs[c]			
Loan Forgiveness for Service in Areas of National Need[d]	Multiple	Multiple	N
Pediatric Subspecialist LRP	Multiple	Single	N
Nursing Workforce Development Student Loans: Loan Cancellation[d]	Multiple	Single	N
Nursing Workforce Development Student Loans: Loan Repayments[e]	n/a	n/a	Y
Eligible Individual Student Loan Repayment	Multiple	Single	N

Source: CRS analysis of relevant statutory and regulatory provisions and additional resources.

Notes: The acronym "LRP" means "loan repayment program."

a. A program is considered to have been active if, since October 1, 2013, borrowers have been eligible to qualify for or begin qualifying for loan repayment benefits under the program.

b. Appropriations have not been provided since FY2010.

c. A program is considered never to have been active if it has been authorized but has not yet received appropriations.

d. Despite the program's name, this is classified as loan repayment program, because benefits are contingent on discretionary appropriations.

e. This program is only available to individuals who withdraw from nursing programs. They must have been unable to complete their studies, be in exceptionally needy circumstances, and have not resumed their studies within two years after they withdrew.

Table 3 illustrates the variety of employment needs these broad-based loan repayment programs are currently intended to meet. In total, there are 21 such programs, and 18 of these programs are targeted, at least in part, to health-related occupations. Of these health-related occupations programs, seven are intended to specifically address healthcare provider shortages, four to meet health research needs, and four to meet healthcare faculty needs. Other occupations specifically targeted by loan repayment programs to meet broad employment needs include legal occupations and large animal veterinarians who provide emergency services.

In all of the programs detailed in **Table 3**, borrowers need not fulfill their service obligations with a single individual employer. Rather, they may fulfill their service by working for multiple employers within the broader class of employers.[39] Some of these programs, however, require

---

[39] See, for example, "National Institutes of Health Extramural Loan Repayment Program: Health Disparities Research" in **Appendix A**.

borrowers to serve in specific geographic locations, typically underserved rural or disadvantaged areas.[40]

Finally, like the loan forgiveness programs, borrowers participating in loan repayment programs must serve for a minimum period of time. For such programs, service commitments generally last between one and five years.

Loan Repayment Programs to Recruit and Retain Federal Government Employees

Loan repayment programs to recruit and retain federal government employees are generally narrowly targeted to meet agency-specific recruitment and retention needs and are potentially the smallest in scale of the loan repayment and forgiveness programs. Although, for many of these programs, information on the programs' scale (e.g., number of benefit recipients and amount of benefits received) is not readily available, the Office of Personnel Management annually reports on the number of agencies participating in, the number of beneficiaries from, and the amount of benefits received from the Government Employee Student Loan Repayment Program.[41]

Table 4 provides a summary of the various loan repayment programs offered for the purposes of individual federal agencies' recruiting and retaining qualified employees. It highlights whether repayment benefits are available only to borrowers who are employed by a single government agency or if benefits may be offered by multiple agencies. It also highlights whether benefits are available only to borrowers who are employed in a single specified occupation, one of multiple eligible occupations; or if no occupational requirement is specified. In addition, it highlights whether borrowers must qualify based, in part, on their economic circumstances.

The table is organized by operational status of each program, and within each operational subheading, programs are grouped by administering department or agency. As with the loan repayment programs addressing broad employment needs or shortages, these programs are not grouped by the potential scope of availability to borrowers and financial resources used to provide benefits, because such data are inconsistently available across programs.

Table 4. Loan Repayment for Public Service Employment in the Federal Government

Program Requirements and Details

Program	Eligible Employer(s)	Eligible Occupation(s)	Income-Dependent (Y/N)
Currently Active Programs[a]			
LRP for Senate Employees	Multiple[b]	Multiple	N
LRP for House Employees	Multiple[c]	Multiple	N

---

[40] See, for example, "National Health Service Corps Loan Forgiveness Program" in **Appendix A**.

[41] See Office of Personnel Management, *Federal Student Loan Repayment Program: Calendar Year 2012*, Report to Congress, September 2013.

Program	Eligible Employer(s)	Eligible Occupation(s)	Income-Dependent (Y/N)
Congressional Budget Office LRP	Single	Multiple	N
Government Employee Student LRP	Multiple	Multiple	N
Defense Acquisition Workforce LRP	Single	Single	N
Armed Forces LRP: Enlisted Members on Active Duty in Specified Military Specialties	Single	Multiple	N
LRP: Members of the Selected Reserve	Single	Multiple	N
LRP: Health Professions Officers Serving in the Selected Reserve with Wartime Critical Medical Skill Shortages	Single	Single	N
LRP: Chaplains Serving in the Selected Reserve	Single	Single	N
Federal Food, Drug, and Cosmetic Act LRP	Single	Single	N
Education Debt Reduction Program	Single	Single	N
National Institutes of Health Intramural LRP: AIDS Research	Single	Single	N
National Institutes of Health Intramural LRP: General Research	Single	Single	N
National Institutes of Health Intramural LRP: General Research for Accreditation Council for Graduate Medical Education Fellows	Single	Single	N

Program	Eligible Employer(s)	Eligible Occupation(s)	Income-Dependent (Y/N)
National Institutes of Health Intramural LRP: Clinical Researchers from Disadvantaged Backgrounds	Single	Single	N
National and Community Service Grant program, Educational Award	Single	Multiple	N
Previously Active Programs			
Capitol Police LRP[d]	Single	Multiple	N
Centers for Disease Control/Agency for Toxic Substances and Disease Registry Educational Loan Repayment Program[e]	Multiple	Single	N
Never Active Programs[f]			
Indian Health Service: Mental Health Prevention and Treatment LRP	Single	Single	N
Program Information Unavailable[g]			
Armed Forces National Call to Service	Single	Multiple	N
LRP: Commissioned Officers in Specified Health Professions	Single	Single	N
Armed Forces Student Loan Interest Payment Program for Members on Active Duty	Single	Multiple	N
Coast Guard LRP	Single	Multiple	N
National Indian Forest Resources Management Postgraduation Recruitment Assumption of Student Loans	Single	Single	N

Program	Eligible Employer(s)	Eligible Occupation(s)	Income-Dependent (Y/N)
American Indian Agricultural Resource Management Postgraduation Recruitment Assumption of Student Loans	Single	Single	N
Loan Repayment Program for Clinical Researchers from Disadvantaged Backgrounds	Single	Single	N

Source: CRS analysis of relevant statutory and regulatory provisions and additional resources.

Notes: The acronym "LRP" means "loan repayment program."

a. A program is considered to have been active if, since October 1, 2013, borrowers have been eligible to qualify for loan forgiveness benefits under the program.

b. Individuals working for U.S. Senate offices are employed by individual Member or committee offices that may offer loan repayment benefits at their discretion.

c. Individuals working for U.S. House of Representatives offices are employed by individual Member or committee offices that may offer loan repayment benefits at their discretion.

d. Appropriations have not been provided since FY2010.

e. Program authorization expired in FY2002.

f. A programs is considered never to have been active if it has been authorized but has not yet received appropriations.

g. Neither appropriations figures nor information on the availability of benefits to borrowers is available for FY2013. Because such information is unavailable, CRS is unable to determine whether these programs were active as of FY2013.

Table 4 shows the array of federal agencies that are authorized to operate loan repayment programs as a means of recruiting and retaining qualified employees. There are 26 such programs, and of these programs, 8 are used to recruit and retain members of the armed forces, with many of the other programs available at federal agencies to varying degrees.

The programs detailed in **Table 4** vary as to whether benefits are available to any employee within an agency or only to employees in specific occupations at the agency. Several programs are generally open to any agency employee,[42] while others are available to employees employed in fields or occupations designated by the administering agency as hard-to-fill or in-need,[43] and yet others are available to agency employees who are employed in certain fields or occupations.[44]

---

[42] See, for example, "Congressional Budget Office Student Loan Repayment" in **Appendix A.**

[43] See, for example, "Armed Forces Educational Loan Repayment Program: Enlisted Members on Active Duty in Specified Military Specialties" in **Appendix A**.

[44] See, for example, "Defense Acquisition Workforce Student Loan Program" in **Appendix A.**

Finally, like the loan repayment programs to meet broad employment needs or shortages, borrowers participating in loan repayment programs must serve for a minimum period of time. For such programs, service commitments generally are between one and five years.

Borrower's Economic Circumstances

Individuals' economic circumstances may affect eligibility, with several loan forgiveness and loan repayment programs using a borrower's economic circumstances as a criterion to qualify for benefits. There are two primary ways that individuals may qualify for benefits based on their economic circumstances. Some programs allow individuals to qualify for benefits based on their economic circumstances at the time they borrow, while other programs allow individuals to qualify for benefits based on their economic circumstances during the repayment period. In some programs, the borrower's economic circumstance is one factor that is considered alongside others, such as qualifying types of service.

Typically, for programs that extend debt relief to borrowers based on their economic circumstances, individuals may be eligible to receive program benefits if they are from a disadvantaged background (based on family economic circumstances)[45] or if their expected monthly loan payment exceeds a certain percentage of their income.[46]

Amount and Timing of Benefits

Programs can also be categorized by the amount of loan forgiveness or loan repayment benefits provided and the schedule for providing those benefits to qualified borrowers. There are three primary methods used to determine the amount of benefits an individual is eligible to receive and when those benefits are realized. Generally, programs forgive the entire outstanding balance of a borrower's loans or repay either a flat dollar amount specified in the authorizing statute or a percentage of the outstanding loan.

Several programs offer to forgive the entire amount of an individual's outstanding student loans. Typically, in these programs, a borrower is required to make a certain number of payments towards the balance of their student loans, and at the end of a specified period of time, the remaining balance of their outstanding loans is forgiven.[47]

A second way in which benefits may be awarded is by an employer paying repayment benefits in the form of a flat dollar amount, usually either paid as a lump sum or in a series of regular payments (e.g., monthly, yearly).[48] Alternatively, some programs may offer varying flat rates that are available to individuals depending on the specific type of service performed.[49]

---

[45] See, for example, "National Institutes of Health Loan Repayment Program for Clinical Researchers from Disadvantaged Backgrounds" in **Appendix A**.

[46] See, for example, "Income-Based Repayment plan for pre-July 1, 2014 borrowers" in **Appendix A**.

[47] See, for example, "Direct Loan Public Service Loan Forgiveness" in **Appendix A**.

[48] See, for example, "Government Employee Student Loan Repayment Program" in **Appendix A**.

[49] See, for example, "Stafford Loan Forgiveness for Teachers" in **Appendix A**.

Finally, some programs pay a percentage of an individual's outstanding loans,[50] with a handful offering borrowers the greater of a certain percentage of a borrower's outstanding loans or a flat dollar amount or an amount equal to a percentage of their outstanding loans.[51]

Exclusions and Limitations

Many loan forgiveness and loan repayment programs contain provisions that may restrict or limit the availability of benefits in certain circumstances. In general, borrowers who have defaulted on their loans are ineligible for loan forgiveness or loan repayment benefits. Certain programs contain restrictions that prohibit borrowers from also receiving benefits under certain other federal student loan forgiveness or loan repayment programs for the same qualifying service. In some programs, borrowers must be U.S. citizens or nationals to be eligible for benefits. In programs that provide loan repayment benefits concurrent with or prior to the completion of the qualifying service, borrowers may be financially penalized if they do not complete their term of service.

Prohibition of Double Benefits

Many federal loan forgiveness and loan repayment programs prohibit individuals from benefitting from multiple programs for completion of the same service. For instance, the Stafford Loan Forgiveness for Teachers program will not make benefits available to individuals for the same service used to qualify for benefits under the Public Service Loan Forgiveness (PSLF) program, the Loan Forgiveness for Service in Areas of National Need program, or for AmeriCorps Education Awards.[52] Alternatively, in some programs, individuals are ineligible for benefits if they are already receiving benefits under another program, but they may become eligible for program benefits once their obligation under the first program is completed.[53]

Citizenship and Immigration Status

Some programs specifically require that participants be U.S. citizens, nationals, or legal permanent residents.[54] Many programs, on the other hand, do not expressly state such a requirement, but these programs may nonetheless only be available to these groups of individuals based on the type of loan eligible for forgiveness or repayment. For example, federal student loans made under the Higher Education Act (HEA), Title IV programs (e.g., FFEL, Direct Loans, and Perkins Loans) are only available to U.S. citizens, nationals, legal permanent residents, and other specified "eligible noncitizens."[55] Thus, the availability of programs that provide loan

---

[50] See, for example, "Federal Perkins Loan Cancellation" in **Appendix A**.

[51] See, for example, "Armed Forces Educational Loan Repayment Program: Enlisted Members on Active Duty in Specific Military Specialties" in **Appendix A**.

[52] 20 U.S.C. §1078-10(g)(2).

[53] See, for example, "National Institutions of Health Extramural Loan Repayment Program: Health Disparities Research" in **Appendix A**.

[54] See, for example, "Indian Health Service Loan Repayment Program" in **Appendix A**.

[55] Those noncitizens eligible to receive federal student financial aid are: U.S. nationals (including natives of American Samoa and Swains Island); permanent U.S. residents with a green card; individuals with an I-94 Arrival/Departure Record designated showing "refugee," "asylum granted," "Cuban-Haitian Entrant (Status Pending)," "Conditional Entrant" (valid only if issued before April 1, 1980), or "Parolee"; individuals with a T-visa or a T-1 visa; a "battered (continued...)

---

forgiveness or loan repayment benefits only for these types of loans (e.g., the PSLF program, which is only available for Direct Loans) is restricted based on a borrower's citizenship and immigration status.[56]

Defaulted Loans

Depending on the program, the availability of loan forgiveness and loan repayment benefits may be restricted for borrowers who have defaulted on their loans. In some programs, the availability of benefits for borrowers whose loans are in default status depends on certain characteristics of the defaulted loans. For instance, in the Direct Loan Stafford Loan Forgiveness for Teachers program, borrowers are generally ineligible for teacher loan forgiveness on defaulted loans, however, loan forgiveness may be granted to borrowers who have made satisfactory repayment arrangements for their loans. While in the Perkins Loan Cancellation program, borrowers of defaulted loans whose loans have not been accelerated[57] may qualify for loan forgiveness on the same terms as borrowers who have not defaulted, and borrowers of defaulted loans whose loans have been accelerated may qualify for loan forgiveness based on service performed prior to, but not after, the date of acceleration.

Clawback Provisions

Provisions that require recipients of loan forgiveness or loan repayment benefits to pay back the amount of the benefits they received if they fail to complete their service obligations may be referred to as clawback provisions. Such provisions are common in federal loan forgiveness and loan repayment programs. Some clawback provisions only require participants to repay an amount equal to the unearned or disallowed portion of their benefits,[58] while others may require participants to repay an amount equal to the benefit received, plus interest.[59] Moreover, in some programs, clawback provisions may also require beneficiaries to pay punitive fees, in addition to amounts equal to the unearned portion of their benefits.[60] Finally, many programs exempt borrowers from liability for unearned benefits if they become disabled, or upon death.[61]

(...continued)

immigrant-qualified alien" who is a victim of abuse by their citizen or permanent resident spouse or is a child of a person designated as a battered immigrant-qualified alien; and citizens of the Federated States of Micronesia, the Republic of the Marshall Islands, and the Republic of Palau (only eligible for Pell Grants, Federal Supplemental Educational Opportunity Grants, and Federal Work Study). Department of Education, Federal Student Aid, "Many non-U.S. citizens qualify for federal student aid," http://studentaid.ed.gov/eligibility/non-us-citizens.

[56] 20 U.S.C. §1087e(m)(1).

[57] When a loan is accelerated, the institution that made the loan may demand immediate repayment of the entire loan, including any late charges, collection costs, and accrued interest. (34 C.F.R. §674.31(b)(8)).

[58] See, for example, "Armed Forces Educational Loan Repayment Program: Enlisted Members on Active Duty in Specified Military Specialties" in **Appendix A**.

[59] See, for example, "Indian Health Service Loan Repayment Program" in **Appendix A**.

[60] See, for example, "National Health Service Corps Loan Repayment Program" in **Appendix A**.

[61] See, for example, "John R. Justice (JRJ) Loan Repayment for Prosecutors and Public Defenders Program" in **Appendix A** and 42 U.S.C. §3797cc-21(d)(1)(D).

Tax Treatment of Loan Forgiveness and Repayment Benefits

In general, student loan debt (and other types of debt) that is forgiven or repaid on a borrower's behalf is included as part of the individual's gross income for the purposes of federal taxation under the Internal Revenue Code (IRC).[62] However, in certain instances, student loan forgiveness and loan repayment benefits may be excluded from gross income and, therefore, exempt from income tax liability.

Some programs' authorizing statutes specifically state that loan forgiveness or loan repayment under those programs will be excluded from an individual's gross income for purposes of taxation. For instance, the HEA specifies that any part of a Federal Perkins Loan that is forgiven is excluded from gross income.[63]

For programs' with authorizing statutes that do not specifically exclude loan forgiveness or loan repayment benefits from gross income, benefits may still be excluded if certain conditions in IRC §108(f) are met. The loans that are repaid or forgiven must have been borrowed to assist an individual in attending a qualified educational institution and must contain terms providing that some or all of the loan balance will be cancelled for work for a specified amount of time in certain professions or occupations and for any broad class of employers.[64] The loan must also have been made by specified types of lenders, including the federal and state governments. Additionally, IRC §108(f)(4) provides exclusions for the National Health Service Corps Loan Repayment program (NHSCLRP) and state programs eligible to receive funds under the Public Health Service Act (PHSA).

If loan forgiveness or repayment benefits are not specifically excluded from income by statute or if the requirements of IRC §108(f)(4) are not met, individuals are responsible for paying any income tax liability associated with the loan forgiveness or loan repayment benefits received. However, at least 13 loan forgiveness and loan repayment programs provide supplemental funds to borrowers to offset any tax liability incurred as a result of the discharge of their loans.[65]

Many recipients of loan forgiveness and loan repayment benefits can avoid being subject to thousands of dollars in taxation if their benefits are excluded from gross income. At the same time, the Joint Committee on Taxation estimated that approximately $200 million of revenue was lost in FY2013 due to the exclusion from taxation of income attributable to the forgiveness and repayment of student loan debt.[66]

---

[62] IRC §61(a)(12).

[63] 20 U.S.C. §1087ee(a)(5).

[64] Loans made under the FFEL, Direct Loan, and Perkins Loan programs all contain terms that provide that if borrowers work for a specified amount of time in certain professions, for certain broad classes of employers, some or all of the debt may be cancelled. Borrowers may also refinance existing loans borrowed from *any* lender by obtaining new loans from qualifying educational or other tax-exempt organizations in order to participate in a public service program offered by that organization. The public service program must be designed to encourage individuals to serve in specific occupations and in which the services performed are under the direction of a governmental or tax-exempt organization. If borrowers refinance their loans in this way, any loan forgiveness or repayment benefits received may be excluded from gross income.

[65] See, for example, "NIH Extramural Loan Repayment Program: Health Disparities Research," in **Appendix A**.

[66] Joint Committee on Taxation, Estimates of Federal Tax Expenditures for Fiscal Years 2012-2017, JCS-1-13, February 1, 2013, p. 37, https://www.jct.gov/publications html?func=startdown&id=4503.

Effectiveness of Loan Forgiveness and Loan Repayment Programs

Researchers debate whether providing loan repayment or forgiveness benefits is an effective way to encourage borrowers to enter specific professional or occupational fields, serve in specific geographic areas, or enter into government service. In general, two main issues are considered when determining the effectiveness of these programs:

1. Whether individuals would enter these fields or take these positions without the prospect for loan forgiveness or loan repayment.

2. Whether student loan debt is the only or the most substantial impediment to entering these fields or taking these positions.

These issues largely focus on the individuals who receive loan forgiveness or loan repayment benefits,[67] but another aspect of effectiveness to consider is the cost of these programs to the federal government relative to the benefits received. The analysis below first discusses program effectiveness as it relates to individuals and is then followed by a discussion of the costs that the federal government incurs when operating loan forgiveness and loan repayment programs.

Evidence of Effectiveness or Ineffectiveness

In assessing the effectiveness of a loan forgiveness or loan repayment program, one issue to consider is whether, in the absence of such a program, the recipient would have engaged in the qualifying service. Information on the effectiveness of such programs might be gleaned from an examination that compares the career paths of individuals who have access to loan forgiveness or loan repayment benefits with the career paths of otherwise similar individuals without such access. These types of evaluations generally have not been conducted for federal loan forgiveness and loan repayment programs. However, some data from one federal program may be instructive.

The National Institutes of Health (NIH) examined the career trajectories of loan repayment recipients in its Intramural Research Program (IRP) and compared them with similar individuals who did not receive loan repayment under the IRP. The purposes of the IRP's loan repayment component is to encourage individuals to complete medical research at the NIH and to encourage qualified health professionals to continue careers in medical research in general (e.g., at a university). The NIH found that individuals receiving loan repayment benefits were more likely to continue conducting medical research at the NIH, and individuals who received loan repayment benefits but then left the NIH were more likely to continue a career as a medical researcher.[68] This study suggests that the program may be meeting its stated goals.

---

[67] The majority of research has examined loan repayment programs. In general, loan forgiveness programs occur after an individual has completed a period of service, thereby, rewarding an individual for choosing a specific occupation. This differs from loan repayment programs that provide repayment during or shortly after an individual is working in a specific occupation or geographic location.

[68] Steven Glazerman and Neil Seftor, *The NIH Intramural Research Loan Repayment Program: Career Outcomes of Participants and Nonparticipants*, Mathematica Policy Research, Inc., Final Report, Washington, DC, November 30, 2005, http://www.lrp.nih.gov/pdf/Intramural_LRP_Outcomes_Evaluation.pdf (hereinafter Glazerman, *NIH Intramural Research Loan Repayment Program*).

While the NIH study indicates that its loan repayment program may be meeting its stated goals, the loan repayment program is unlikely the sole reason for at least some of the individuals to remain in the NIH's targeted positions. Other research has found that some individuals would have entered certain fields or taken certain positions in the absence of loan repayments for a variety of other reasons. If this were true, then the program would not have been necessary and, therefore, might be considered ineffective. For example, recent research has found that government positions are rather desirable.[69] If this is the case, then a loan repayment program to induce individuals into government service may not be necessary. Similarly, a loan repayment program may be an effective incentive when jobs are plentiful for recent graduates but may not be necessary when there are fewer employment opportunities. In recent years, for example, law school graduates have had fewer employment opportunities[70] and may take a public interest or government job because of more limited private sector opportunities. Finally, individuals who accept loan repayment for a specific job may have taken the same job without loan repayment benefits. For example, one study found that health providers who practice in rural areas would have done so without receiving a loan repayment award.[71]

Although in some cases loan forgiveness or loan repayment programs may appear to be unnecessary, in some instances there is evidence showing that participants would likely not have taken a particular position but for loan repayment. For example, the NIH examined its IRP loan repayment program and found that most loan repayment award recipients had competing job offers and stated that the potential for loan repayment was an attractive benefit that was unique to the NIH employment. This was particularly true for physicians who often had competing job offers at higher salaries. Physicians who received loan repayment benefits were also more likely to remain in research at the NIH, which demonstrates that loan repayment may be an important recruitment and retention tool.[72]

Other federal agencies have found that loan repayment programs are effective at recruiting and maintaining staff, but there are indications that some aspects of a program's design may undermine its effectiveness.[73] For example, discretionary programs may have their funding reduced or cut altogether, thus making the availability of loan repayment benefits to individuals uncertain. The effectiveness of these programs as a recruitment incentive may be hard to determine because job applicants do not know whether they will receive a loan repayment award until after having accepted a job.[74] Additionally, loan repayment award amounts may not be a sufficient incentive, because participants are often responsible for the federal income taxes associated with receiving the loan repayment. Specifically, under the Government Employee Student Loan Repayment Program (GESLRP), participants are responsible for the tax liability,

---

[69] For instance, in 2012, American students ranked 12 federal agencies among the top 100 ideal employers. Universum, *America's Ideal Employers 2012*, 2012, http://www.universumglobal.com/IDEAL-Employer-Rankings/The-National-Editions/American-Student-Survey.

[70] National Association for Legal Career Professionals, *Class of 2011 Has Lowest Employment Rate Since Class of 1994*, NALP Bulletin, July 2012, http://www.nalp.org/0712research.

[71] D.M. Renner et al., "The Influence of Loan Repayment on Rural Healthcare Provider Recruitment and Retention in Colorado," *Rural and Remote Health*, vol. 10, no. 1605 (September 4, 2010).

[72] Glazerman, *NIH Intramural Research Loan Repayment Program*.

[73] U.S. Government Accountability Office, *Federal Student Loan Repayment Program: OPM Could Build on Its Efforts to Help Agencies Administer the Program and Measure Results*, 05-762, July 22, 2005.

[74] Glazerman, *NIH Intramural Research Loan Repayment Program*.

---

which some agencies estimate can account for 39% of the loan repayment amount. Some agencies suggest that this makes the program less attractive to participants.[75]

The second major issue regarding the assessment of loan forgiveness and loan repayment programs is whether it is accurate to assume that individuals would otherwise enter a certain field or take a specific job but for their student loan debt. Loan forgiveness and loan repayment programs are predicated on the assumption that student loan debt is a large factor in making employment decisions. However, researchers have found that career choices are more complex; that debt, in some instances, may have little or no effect on career or job choices; and that a number of other deterrents may reduce student interest in a specific field or may make students less likely to seek employment in certain geographic areas.[76] For example, the National Health Service Corps Loan Repayment Program (NHSCLRP) provides loan repayment benefits to physicians (among other health professionals) who enter primary care and practice in specific geographic areas. Although lower levels of compensation are one deterrent that keep physicians from entering primary care medicine, physicians might not enter these fields for other reasons as well. For instance, a physician may prefer to focus in a specialty or may not want to assume the increased administrative duties that primary care physicians incur.[77] Moreover, others have found that debt levels may play a greater role in career decisions for certain racial and ethnic groups.[78] Because it may be difficult or undesirable to target programs by racial and ethnic group, loan forgiveness and loan repayment programs may be available to individuals for whom debt is not a factor in career choice.

A related critique of loan forgiveness and loan repayment programs is that despite these programs' providing a financial inducement for individuals to enter a specific field that is relatively lower paying (e.g., primary care medicine versus a specialty field), the amount received is generally far less than the overall lifetime earnings gap. One study estimated that over a lifetime, the average primary care physician earns $3.5 million less than a specialty physician.[79] Given that borrowers are unlikely to have $3.5 million in student loan debt, loan repayments cannot fully make up for the lower lifetime earnings from entering primary care.

Other research has found that high levels of debt do influence job choice. For example, in a literature review of the influence of law school debt on legal practice, the author found that high levels of law school debt often make it more likely for recent graduates to work at large law firms, where they are likely to earn more.[80] Similarly, when examining the career trajectories of

---

[75] Ibid.

[76] Robert L. Phillips, Jr. et al., *Specialty and Geographic Distribution of the Physician Workforce: What Influences Medical Student and Resident Choices?*, Robert Graham Center and Josiah B. Macy Foundation, Washington, DC, March 2, 2009, http://www.graham-center.org/online/etc/medialib/graham/documents/publications/mongraphs-books/2009/rgcmo-specialty-geographic.Par.0001.File.tmp/Specialty-geography-compressed.pdf.

[77] U.S. Government Accountability Office, Graduate Medical Education: Trends in Training and Student Debt, 09-438R, May 4, 2009, http://www.gao.gov/new.items/d09438r.pdf.

[78] The Committee on Legal Education and Admission to the Bar, "Law School Debt and the Practice of Law," *The Record of the Association of the City of New York*, 2003.

[79] The Council on Graduate Medical Education, Twentieth Report, Advancing Primary Care, Rockville, MD, December 2010.

[80] Erica Field, "Educational Debt Burden and Career Choice: Evidence from a Financial Aid Experiment at NYU Law School," *American Economic Journal: Applied Economics*, vol. 1, no. 1 (January 2009), pp. 1-21. This study also examined how the design of a law school's loan repayment program also influenced its effectiveness. Specifically, the author found that scholarship programs were more effective for encouraging students to enter public interest law when compared to loan repayment programs.

undergraduates, researchers have found that undergraduate students with higher debt levels are more likely to choose higher salary jobs and less likely to enter education-related fields, work for a government agency, or work at a nonprofit organization—all job choices that traditionally are associated with a lower income than their private sector counterparts.[81] Some studies, however, have found that law school debt levels may play a secondary role in an individual's determination of which occupations to enter after graduation, while demographic characteristics may be a more dominant factor in the decision-making process (similar to the finding noted above that there is racial and ethnic variation in the importance of debt on career trajectories). This may indicate that loan repayment programs have little or no effect on the career choice of law school graduates.[82]

From an employer's perspective (which, for many of the currently existing programs is the federal government) effectiveness may be measured in terms of their ability to obtain a more skilled workforce than would exist without such programs. For example, one study found that a loan repayment program administered by the Army was important in retaining dentists.[83] However, it is also possible that these programs also provide a less stable workforce. Although the goal of a number of federal programs is to recruit and retain a highly skilled workforce who may not otherwise enter public service, many of these same programs may only be providing short-term benefits (e.g., two years' worth of loan repayment benefits) that may contribute to turnover, as individuals may decide to change jobs once they have realized the full benefit of a program. For example, some researchers have found that individuals who have a service obligation have shorter tenures in a particular position than do individuals who do not have service obligations.[84]

Cost of Loan Forgiveness and Loan Repayment Programs

The granting of loan forgiveness and loan repayment benefits to borrowers results in costs to the federal government. The nature of the costs that are incurred by the government depends on the structure of the applicable program through which these benefits are made available. There are three categories of costs that typically may be associated with loan forgiveness and loan repayment programs: loan subsidy costs, appropriated program costs, and administrative costs.

Loan Subsidy Costs

Loan forgiveness programs typically make available benefits that are incorporated into the terms and conditions of loans that are made through federal student loan programs and which are classified as federal credit programs for federal budgeting purposes. Federal credit consists of

---

[81] Jesse Rothstein and Cecilia Elena Rouse, "Constrained After College: Student Loans and Early Career Occupational Choices," *Journal of Public Economics,* 95(1-2) (February 2011), pp. 149-163.

[82] The Committee on Legal Education and Admission to the Bar, "Law School Debt and the Practice of Law," *The Record of the Association of the City of New York*, 2003.

[83] Nasrin Mazujii et al., "Army Junior Dental Officer Retention," *Military Medicine*, vol. 170 (January 2005), pp. 21-25.

[84] Till Barnighausen and David E. Bloom, "Financial Incentives for Return of Service in Underserved Areas: A Systematic Review," *BMC Health Services Research*, vol. 9, no. 86 (May 29, 2009).

federal direct loans and federal loan guarantees.[85] The William D. Ford Federal Direct Loan program is a direct loan program, and the Federal Family Education Loan (FFEL) program is a guaranteed loan program. Loan subsidy costs for these programs are funded through mandatory indefinite appropriations. According to requirements of the Federal Credit Reform Act of 1990 (FCRA),[86] the budgetary costs of direct loans and loan guarantees are measured on the basis of their estimated loan-term costs to the government on a present value basis and these costs are attributable to the fiscal year during which a direct loan obligation or guaranteed loan commitment is made (as opposed to the year during which the cash flows associated with these benefits occur). The federal budget reflects the unreimbursed costs of making or guaranteeing loans—the subsidy cost of loans (discussed below) and administrative costs (which are expressed separately on a cash basis, and discussed in a following section).[87]

The loan subsidy cost is the estimated present value of the cash flows from the government (excluding administrative expenses), less the estimated present value of the cash flows to the government, resulting from a direct loan or loan guarantee, and discounted to the time when the loan is disbursed. A positive loan subsidy cost means that there is a cost to the government of providing the loan subsidy to borrowers. A negative loan subsidy cost means that the government earns a positive return from the extension of credit to borrowers. With regard to loan forgiveness benefits that are incorporated into the terms and conditions of direct loan or guaranteed loan programs, the availability (and eventual granting) of these benefits alters the expected cash flows of the program and results in an increase in loan subsidy costs.[88]

For example, in the Direct Loan program, Stafford Loan Forgiveness to Teachers is a benefit that is made available to qualified borrowers. When borrowers qualify for loan forgiveness under the program, a portion of each borrower's loan balance (e.g., $5,000, $17,500) is discharged by the government. As a consequence, these borrowers are relieved of responsibility for repaying some portion of their loans and the cash flows to the government associated with these loans are reduced. This results in an increase in loan subsidy costs for the program. While these loan forgiveness benefits may not be provided until many years after a loan is made, the estimated cost of providing these loan forgiveness benefits is accounted for in the loan subsidy costs for the fiscal year during which the loan was originally made. Other examples of this type of program include the Public Service Loan Forgiveness (PSLF) program and loan forgiveness following completion of the maximum repayment period (e.g., 20 years, 25 years) in the income-based repayment (IBR) plan and the income-contingent repayment (ICR) plan.

---

[85] In a federal direct loan program, the federal government directly lends federal funds to a borrower. In a federal loan guarantee program, the federal government guarantees lenders against loss through borrower default, death, permanent disability, or, in limited circumstances, bankruptcy.

[86] Title V of P.L. 101-508.

[87] For additional background on federal credit programs, see CRS Report R42632, *Budgetary Treatment of Federal Credit (Direct Loans and Loan Guarantees): Concepts, History, and Issues for Congress*, by Mindy R. Levit; and Office of Management and Budget, Budget of the United States Government, Fiscal Year 2015, Analytical Perspectives, "Budget Concepts and Budget Process: Federal Credit," pp. 101-102, http://www.whitehouse.gov/sites/default/files/omb/budget/fy2015/assets/concepts.pdf.

[88] Loan subsidy costs are estimated for each cohort of loans and these rates are reestimated annually while loans in the cohort are still outstanding. A final accounting of loan subsidies is not available until loans in the cohort are no longer outstanding.

Appropriated Program Costs

In loan repayment programs, the direct costs of borrower benefits are not incorporated into the subsidy rates of the federal credit programs through which the federal student loans were made, but rather are funded through the appropriation of funds for the fiscal year during which the loan repayment benefits are made available. (However, the early repayment of a loan may have an effect on loan subsidy costs.) Funding may be provided through either discretionary or mandatory appropriations. For these types of programs, benefits are available to borrowers only in years for which appropriations have been made and only to the extent that the availability of funds allows. Thus, for these types of programs, sufficient funding might not be available to extend benefits to all borrowers who satisfy the eligibility criteria for loan repayment benefits. Examples of programs funded through discretionary appropriations include the Government Employee Student Loan Repayment (GESLR) program and the John R. Justice (JRJ) Loan Repayment for Prosecutors and Public Defenders Program. An example of a program funded through mandatory appropriations is the National Health Service Corps Loan Repayment program (NHSCLRP).

The manner of providing funding for Perkins Loan Cancellation benefits is unique. The availability of Perkins Loan Cancellation benefits is specified in the terms and conditions of Perkins Loans and all borrowers who satisfy program eligibility criteria must be granted loan forgiveness by the institution that made the Perkins Loan. However, whereas most loan forgiveness program benefits are components of federal credit programs, the Perkins Loan program is not a federal credit program. Funding for Perkins Loan Cancellation benefits is authorized to be made available through discretionary appropriations. While funding was last appropriated for Perkins Loan Cancellation reimbursements in FY2009, qualified borrowers have continued to have their loans canceled despite no funding being appropriated. Since the Perkins Loan program is a revolving loan fund program, institutions that have canceled Perkins Loans for eligible borrowers have absorbed the costs of loan cancellation without having these costs reimbursed by the federal government. ED currently maintains a record of reimbursement amounts institutions would be eligible to receive should funding be appropriated.[89]

Administrative Costs

Whereas most of the costs associated with loan forgiveness and loan repayment programs may be considered programmatic costs and are either incorporated into loan subsidy rates or are funded on a fiscal year basis through discretionary or mandatory appropriations for the applicable program, the costs of administering these programs are generally accounted for and funded separately. For loan forgiveness benefits that are offered through federal credit programs, in accordance with requirements of the FCRA, administrative costs are accounted for separately on a cash basis and are funded through annual appropriations. Loan repayment programs are administered by numerous agencies and there is variation across programs in how administrative costs are funded. For ED programs administered by Federal Student Aid, discretionary appropriations are provided for federal student aid administration.

---

[89] U.S. Department of Education, Office of Federal Student Aid, Electronic Announcement, "2011-2012 Federal Perkins Loan Service Cancellation Reimbursement," April 24, 2013.

Estimated and Actual Costs for Loan Forgiveness and Loan Repayment Programs

Limited information is available on the actual costs to the government of loan forgiveness and loan repayment programs. For some programs—particularly many loan forgiveness programs—the only information available on program costs are estimates of the dollar amount or number of loans projected to be forgiven in future years, because borrowers have not yet become eligible to realize these benefits. For other programs—primarily loan repayment programs—information is often available on items such as the total amount of benefits provided or the number of borrowers who received benefits in a given fiscal year. Cost estimates for loan forgiveness programs in which benefits have not yet been realized are discussed below. For a limited set of programs in which benefits have been awarded to borrowers, and where relevant data are available, data on the amount of debt relief provided and the number of recipients is presented in **Appendix A** on a program-by-program basis.

Cost Estimates for Selected Loan Forgiveness Programs

For the Direct Loan Public Service Loan Forgiveness program, in a 2008 notice of proposed rulemaking (NPRM) to implement changes made by the College Cost Reduction and Access Act of 2007 (P.L. 110-84), ED estimated a cost to the government of $1.5 billion over the five-year period of FY2008-2012, with $1.2 billion of that amount being associated with loans made prior to FY2008.[90] (For federal credit programs, costs are associated with the cohort year in which a loan is made, as opposed to the year in which benefits are realized.) ED did not provide estimates of the number of borrowers expected to receive loan forgiveness benefits.

For the Pay-As-You-Earn (PAYE) repayment plan, in a 2012 NPRM, ED estimated a cost to the government of $2.1 billion over the ten-year period of FY2012-2021. In arriving at this figure, ED estimated that approximately 1.67 million borrowers would elect to repay their loans according to the PAYE plan. Of these borrowers, ED estimated that approximately 400,000 would receive loan forgiveness through either public service loan forgiveness or after 20 years of repayment according to the PAYE plan.[91] On a per-borrower basis, ED estimated that the average original loan balance of borrowers receiving loan forgiveness would be $39,500 and that, because many borrowers would pay only interest and no principal on their loans under the PAYE plan, these borrowers would have an average of $41,000 in loans forgiven.[92]

For the IBR plan, in its 2008 NPRM, ED estimated that 126,000 borrowers from the FY2009 loan cohort would repay their loans according to IBR, and that 44,000 of such borrowers would have at least some portion of their student loan debt forgiven after 25 years. For the FY2012 cohort, ED estimated that 146,000 borrowers would repay according to the IBR plan, and that 52,000 of these borrowers would have some portion of their debt forgiven after 25 years.[93]

---

[90] U.S. Department of Education, "Federal Perkins Loan Program, Federal Family Education Loan Program, and William D. Ford Federal Direct Loan Program; Proposed Rule," 73 *Federal Register* 127, July 1, 2008, p. 37709.

[91] U.S. Department of Education, "Federal Perkins Loan Program, Federal Family Education Loan Program, and William D. Ford Federal Direct Loan Program; Proposed Rule ," 77 *Federal Register* 137, July 17, 2012, p. 42121.

[92] Ibid., p. 42122.

[93] Ibid., p. 33709.

Given that many of these loan forgiveness benefits are relatively new, and that both loan forgiveness receipt and benefit amounts are contingent upon borrower repayment behavior and/or labor market experiences over a sustained period of time, it is likely difficult to precisely estimate loan forgiveness benefits in aggregate.

Issues for Congress

Congress may explore whether existing policy on the availability of federal student loan forgiveness and loan repayment programs is optimal or whether changes should be made. Several issues related to loan forgiveness and loan repayment policy might be examined. For instance, should multiple programs make available loan forgiveness or loan repayment benefits for borrowers who engage in similar types of activities? Does the structure of some loan forgiveness or loan repayment programs lead to a financial windfall for borrowers who engage in the same type of activity they otherwise would have even if debt relief were not available? Is sufficient information available to assess whether existing programs are effectively achieving their intended purposes?

Overlapping of Benefits Across Programs

Programs may be considered to overlap if multiple programs have the same or substantially similar goals and activities. There are two primary ways that student loan forgiveness and repayment programs can be considered overlapping. First, the same borrower could receive benefits from two different programs for the same service performed. Second, multiple programs may be available to the same group of individuals and may serve the same purpose, such that the federal government could be spending money on administrative costs for both programs when only one may be sufficient.

Individuals potentially may be able to qualify for benefits under multiple programs. Although some programs (e.g., Stafford Loan Forgiveness for Teachers) specifically state that recipients are not allowed to receive benefits under that and certain other programs for the same qualifying service, some programs do not contain such restrictions. Without such limitations, recipients may be able to receive benefits from multiple sources for the same service performed. For instance, an individual working in a federal agency may be eligible to receive up to $10,000 per year in loan repayment benefits (and up to $60,000 in total) under the Government Employee Student Loan Repayment program (GESLRP), while concurrently qualifying for forgiveness of the remainder of their student loan debt after 10 years of service with a federal agency and 120 concurrent monthly loan payments under the Public Service Loan Forgiveness program (PSLF).[94] If the individual applied the benefits received under the GESLRP towards the 120 monthly payments necessary to qualify for loan forgiveness under the PSLF, he or she potentially would be receiving benefits under two programs for the same federal government service.[95]

Another way in which programs can overlap is that multiple programs may be available to the same groups of individuals. Here, the federal government may be funding administrative costs for

---

[94] 5 U.S.C. §5379; 20 U.S.C. §1087e(m).

[95] In such a case, individuals are not making a profit. Rather, they are having more of their loans paid off than is typically expected as a part of these programs.

two separate programs that are serving the same purpose or same group of people. The Nursing Education Loan Repayment Program (NELRP), for instance, provides repayment benefits to, among others, individuals who serve as nurse faculty at accredited nursing schools.[96] The Nursing Faculty Loan Repayment Program (NFLRP) is available to individuals who serve as nurse faculty at accredited nursing schools.[97] Both programs are intended to increase the number of qualified nursing faculty, and both programs are administered by the Department of Health and Human Services, Health Resources and Services Administration (HRSA). However, under the NFLRP, the HRSA grants money to nursing schools that establish their own loan repayment programs and then choose which individuals may receive benefits. These programs may be creating a burden on the HRSA if it is responsible for administering both the NELRP and also granting money to the NFLRP when both programs are available to the same group of individuals and are intended to serve the same purpose.

Congress may consider combining, altering, or abolishing programs that either make available double benefits to individuals for the same service or that are available to the same group of individuals and intended to serve the same purpose.

Debt Relief or Windfall?

Many loan forgiveness and repayment programs are intended to encourage individuals to enter into specified jobs, careers, or public service that may otherwise be undesirable or hard-to-fill. While this may be an effective way of recruiting and retaining some individuals who might not have otherwise considered entering such fields, these programs could be providing windfalls for other individuals who would have entered the field regardless of benefit availability.

For instance, there are no limits on the amounts that may be forgiven under certain loan forgiveness plans (e.g., the Direct Loan Public Service Loan Forgiveness program and loan forgiveness following income-dependent repayment). Notably, the Direct Loan Public Service Loan Forgiveness program operates in conjunction with the income-dependent repayment plans. Concerns are beginning to be raised that certain characteristics of these programs, combined with the large amounts that individuals may borrow—particularly amounts borrowed under non-need-based PLUS Loans made to graduate and professional students—may create situations in which individuals may borrow larger amounts than they otherwise would, knowing that the possibility exists for loan forgiveness.[98] Congress may consider whether limits should be established on amounts that may be forgiven under certain loan forgiveness programs.[99]

The GESLRP is used by some federal government agencies to recruit and retain qualified employees. While this may have been an effective tool for recruiting employees at a time when federal government employment was often seen as less desirable than nonfederal employment, such benefits might be construed as creating windfalls, as employment with the federal

---

[96] 42 U.S.C. §297n

[97] 42 U.S.C. §297n-1.

[98] Jason Delisle and Alex Holt, "Safety Net or Windfall? Examining Changes to Income-Based Repayment for Federal Student Loans," New America Foundation, October 2012.

[99] For example, in his FY2015 Budget, President Obama has proposed capping the amount that may be forgiven under the Direct Loan Public Service Loan Forgiveness program at $57,500. (See U.S. Department of Education, *FY 2015 Department of Education Justifications of Appropriation Estimates to the Congress*, Student Loans Overview, p. S-15).

government is now considered by many to be attractive.[100] Additionally, some studies suggest that many entry-level, federal government new hires specifically sought federal employment during their job search.[101] Borrowers may want to work in the federal government, regardless of whether loan repayment is offered. However, once they are employed with the federal government, they may participate in a loan repayment program if it is available to them, even though program availability may not have played a role in their decision to work for, or remain employed by, the federal government.

If the goal of loan forgiveness and loan repayment programs is to immediately place individuals in or attract highly skilled employees to specified occupations or service and they are already seeking employment within such fields, then the programs may be considered ineffective, as they may not have played a role in individual employment decisions. However, if the goal of these programs is to create pipelines for future careers or retain highly skilled employees, then the programs may be somewhat effective, as some studies indicate that loan repayment programs do play at least some role in an individual's choice in staying in a specific job or career.[102]

To tailor loan repayment programs to more specific needs, Congress may consider implementing more sensitive funding controls, such as more narrowly defining the circumstances in which individuals could become eligible for repayment benefits, rather than giving administering agencies broad discretion in implementation. Alternatively, since many programs are funded through discretionary appropriations, Congress could also direct the use of funds through language included in appropriations measures.

Data on Program Outcomes and Effectiveness

In general, insufficient data are available on federal loan forgiveness and loan repayment programs to assess their effectiveness in achieving program objectives. For many programs, only a limited amount of programmatic data is available. For others, data will only become available once borrowers apply for and receive benefits. Since, for some programs, the period to qualify for benefits spans many years and no benefits have yet been awarded, limited or no programmatic data are available. For example, in the PSLF program, borrowers must remain employed in a public service job for 10 years while making 120 monthly payments on their loans. This program was established in 2007 and borrowers will not begin to apply for and receive benefits until 2017. Borrowers may, but are not required to, document their employment in public service jobs on PSLF Employment Certification Forms filed with the Department of Education (ED). Thus, information available for this program may provide a snapshot of interest in PSLF, but little more. Loan forgiveness is also available for borrowers who repay according to the income-dependent repayment plans (e.g., income-based repayment (ICR) plan and income-based repayment (IBR)

---

[100] See, for example, Partnership for Public Service and The National Association of Colleges and Employers, *College Students Are Attracted to Federal Service, but Agencies Need to Capitalize on Their Interest*, Issue Brief, March 2014.

[101] Merit Systems Protection Board, *Attracting the Next Generation: A Look at Federal Entry-Level New Hires*, Washington, DC, January 8, 2008, p. 32, http://www.mspb.gov/netsearch/viewdocs.aspx?docnumber=314895& version=315306&application=ACROBAT.

[102] Office of Personnel Management, *Federal Student Loan Repayment Program Calendar Year 2012*, Report to Congress, Washington, DC, September 2013, p. 8, http://www.opm.gov/policy-data-oversight/pay-leave/student-loan-repayment/reports/2012.pdf (hereinafter OPM, *Federal Student LRP*); Glazerman, *NIH Intramural Research Loan Repayment Program*.

plan) for extended periods (e.g., 25 or 20 years). However, these programs also have not been in existence long enough for borrowers to qualify for forgiveness benefits.

For many programs, longitudinal data are not collected on participants beyond what is necessary for program administration. Thus, while data may be available to verify that a borrower remained employed in a targeted position long enough to qualify for benefits, it may be difficult to determine whether a beneficiary remained in his or her position after the qualifying period of employment ended. Where data are collected and available, the data may provide information on program outcomes, but may be of limited use in assessing program effectiveness. While improved data collection and reporting may be resource intensive, the improved availability of information may be necessary for determining program effectiveness and whether program design changes could improve effectiveness.[103]

Qualifying Loan Types and Amounts

There is variation from program to program in the types and amounts of student loan debt that may qualify for debt relief. For some programs, debt relief is limited to specific loan types (e.g., Perkins Loan cancellation), or to specific amounts (e.g., $5,000 or $17,500 for Stafford Teacher Loan Forgiveness). While for other programs, debt relief is available for multiple loan types (e.g., John R. Justice (JRJ) Loan Repayment), or with few limitations on maximum amounts (e.g., PSLF and loan forgiveness following IBR).

Consideration might be given to whether additional limitations should be imposed on the types and amounts of student loan debt that qualifies under loan forgiveness and loan repayment programs. For instance, in recent years, amounts that students may borrow in non-need-based loan aid have increased substantially—particularly due to PLUS Loans being made available to graduate and professional student borrowers. Should individuals continue to be permitted to borrow non-need-based federal student loans to finance expenses that, according to federal need analysis rules, would otherwise be met by their expected family contribution (EFC), and then have a substantial portion of that amount discharged through federal student loan forgiveness or loan repayment programs? Should limits be established on the amount or type of student loan debt that may qualify for debt relief?

Variability of Selection Criteria Among Administering Agencies

Selection criteria among agencies administering student loan repayment programs can vary greatly.[104] For example, the GESLRP permits federal agencies to administer their own student loan repayment programs so long as they meet basic statutory requirements. Because of this, selection criteria may be unpredictable throughout the federal government, and in some cases, agencies may not administer a repayment program at all. In calendar year (CY) 2012, of the many

---

[103] It would take evaluation, however, to assess what would have happened in the absence of the availability of benefits.

[104] For a table summarizing how many of the federal agencies administer their programs, see, U.S. Government Accountability Office, *Federal Student Loan Repayment Program: OPM Could Build on Its Efforts to Help Agencies Administer the Program and Measure Results*, 05-762, July 22, 2005, p. 16, Table 1, http://www.gao.gov/assets/250/247197.pdf.

federal agencies, 35 agencies provided employees with loan repayment benefits under the GESLRP.[105]

Under the GESLRP, participants in any agency must sign a service agreement to serve in the paying agency for at least three years and they must reimburse a paying agency for any benefits received if they do not complete their service. Also, participants cannot be employees in the excepted service due to their position being confidential, policy-determining, policy-making, or policy-advocating in nature.[106] Beyond these limitations, however, agencies can otherwise determine to whom benefits are given. The Department of Defense, for example, uses its program extensively to recruit employees in engineering positions.[107] The U.S. Agency for International Development, on the other hand, requires that individuals meet certain position and pay grade conditions to be eligible for benefits.[108]

Although individual agencies can tailor their specific loan repayment program to meet their unique needs, these variations throughout a single government-wide program can make eligibility requirements difficult for participants to discern. If the goal of the program is to attract qualified individuals to work in the federal government, the GESLRP may only attract individuals to work in a limited number of agencies that administer the program.[109]

---

[105] OPM, *Federal Student LRP*, p. 4.

[106] 5 U.S.C. §5379(a)(2).

[107] OPM, *Federal Student LRP*, p. 6.

[108] U.S. Agency for International Development, "Foreign Service Officer FAQ," http://www.usaid.gov/work-usaid/careers/foreign-service/foreign-service-officer-faq.

[109] Moreover, because each agency's funding levels differ and the GESLRP is a discretionary program that may have its funding reduced or cut altogether, the availability of benefits to individuals among agencies may be uncertain, and applicants may not know whether they will receive benefits until after accepting a job. Glazerman, *NIH Intramural Research Loan Repayment Program*.

Appendix A. Program-Specific Details

The following appendix provides program-specific details about each program included in this report's analysis. Efforts were made to present the information in a relatively consistent manner; however, the programs are sufficiently different that information varies in scope and level of detail.

For each program, the following information, where available, is provided:

- Statutory and regulatory citations and Catalog of Federal Domestic Assistance (CFDA) number(s);

- The federal administering agency and (where appropriate) the specific office within that agency;

- The program's purpose;

- Types of loans eligible for forgiveness or repayment;

- Qualifying service required of program participants;

- Maximum amount of benefits program participants can receive;

- Restrictions on eligibility for program benefits;

- Requirements for program participants after receipt of all or part of a program's benefits;

- Federal income tax treatment of benefits;

- Budgetary classification of the program's spending;

- Annual amounts appropriated in FY2009-FY2013;

- Annual amount of loans discharged or repaid in FY2009-FY2013;

- Annual number of program beneficiaries in FY2009-FY2013; and

- Citations to relevant CRS reports and additional resources.

Information was derived from statutes, regulations, agency websites, or other authoritative sources.

Only selected information that is relevant to the overall analysis of this report is included in these program descriptions. Programs are described as they exist in FY2014. For complete information about a particular program of interest, readers are referred to the legal citations provided, the federal administering agency, or the identified CRS report. A notation of "N/A" indicates that criteria are not applicable to a specific program. Abbreviations used throughout this appendix include Federal Family Education Loan (FFEL) and Public Health Service Act (PHSA).

The various programs are presented in the same order as discussed earlier in this report. Loan forgiveness programs for public service are presented first. These are followed by programs that offer forgiveness following income-dependent repayment. Next, loan repayment programs for public service addressing broad employment needs or shortages are presented. Loan repayment programs for public service employment in the federal government are presented last.

Loan Forgiveness for Public Service Employment Programs

The loan forgiveness programs presented in this section provide debt relief to qualified borrowers employed in certain occupations, for specific employers, or in public service. These benefits are considered entitlements and are written into the terms and conditions of widely available federal student loans. They are potentially available to an open-ended number of qualified borrowers and are presented first in this appendix, as they have a potentially large scope of availability to borrowers.

Direct Loan Public Service Loan Forgiveness (PSLF) program

Authority: Statute: HEA, Title IV, §455(m); 20 U.S.C. §1087e(m). *Regulations:* 34 C.F.R. §§685.212(i) & 685.219. *CFDA:* 84.268.

Federal administering agency: U.S. Department of Education, Federal Student Aid.

Purpose or description of program: To provide student loan forgiveness for the balance of any principal and interest that remains due on the Direct Loan program loans of borrowers who, after October 1, 2007, have made 120 full, scheduled, monthly payments (10 years) on those loans, according to certain repayment plans, while concurrently employed full-time in public service.

Eligible loan types: Direct Loan program Subsidized Loans, Unsubsidized Loans, Graduate PLUS Loans, and Consolidation Loans.

Qualifying service or other activity: To qualify for loan forgiveness, borrowers must be employed full-time in public service, which includes employment in public service organizations and service in AmeriCorps or the Peace Corps. Public service organizations are federal, state, local, or tribal government agencies, organizations, or entities; tribal colleges and universities; public child or family service agencies; nonprofit organizations that are tax-exempt under IRC §501(c)(3); and private nonprofit organizations (other than labor unions or partisan political organizations). An eligible public service organization must provide any of the following public services: emergency management, military service, public safety, law enforcement, public interest law services, early childhood education, public service for individuals with disabilities and the elderly, public health, public education, public library services, and school library or other school-based services.

Maximum benefit amount: The maximum amount that may be forgiven is any loan balance that remains after 120 qualifying monthly payments have been made on the loan.

Restrictions on eligibility: Borrowers must make 120 separate, full, on-time, scheduled monthly payments within 15 days of the due date. Each of the payments must be made according to either the income-based repayment (IBR) plan, the income-contingent (ICR) plan, a standard repayment plan with a 10-year repayment period, or another Direct Loan program repayment plan if the payment amounts are equal to or greater than the amount that would be required according to a standard repayment plan with a 10-year repayment period. Borrowers must be employed (or serving) full-time in public service at the time each of the required 120 payments are made, at the time the application for forgiveness is made, and at the time forgiveness is granted. Borrowers' loans may not be in default. Any time spent participating in religious instruction, worship services, or proselytizing may not be included as part of full-time public service at a nonprofit organization.

Post-award conditions: N/A

Federal tax treatment: The amount of student loans forgiven is excluded from gross income.

Budgetary classification and funding: Mandatory. Amounts provided for loan forgiveness are incorporated into student loan subsidy costs.

Amounts discharged or repaid: N/A. Borrowers will first become eligible for loan forgiveness in October 2017.

Annual number of beneficiaries: N/A. Borrowers will first become eligible for loan forgiveness in October 2017.

CRS report: CRS Report R40122, *Federal Student Loans Made Under the Federal Family Education Loan Program and the William D. Ford Federal Direct Loan Program: Terms and Conditions for Borrowers*, by David P. Smole.

Additional resources: U.S. Department of Education, Federal Student Aid, "Public Service Loan Forgiveness," http://www.studentaid.ed.gov/node/91.

Stafford Loan Forgiveness for Teachers

Authority: Statute: HEA, Title IV, §§428J and 460; 20 U.S.C. §§1078-10 and 1087j. *Regulations:* 34 C.F.R. §§682.216, 685.212(h), and 685.217. *CFDA:* 84.032 and 84.268.

Federal administering agency: U.S. Department of Education, Federal Student Aid.

Purpose of program: To encourage individuals to enter into and continue in the teaching profession.

Eligible loan types: FFEL and Direct Loan program Subsidized Loans, Unsubsidized Loans, and Consolidation Loans to the extent used to repay a Subsidized Loan or an Unsubsidized Loan.

Qualifying service or other activity: To qualify for loan repayment benefits, borrowers must serve as full-time teachers for at least five consecutive complete academic years in a public nonprofit school, a private nonprofit school, or a public education service agency (ESA) that serves children from low-income families. For teaching service in a school, at least one of the five school years must be after the 1997-1998 school year, and for teaching service in an ESA, a portion of the five school years must be after the 2007-2008 school year. Borrowers whose five-year service periods began on or after October 30, 2004, must be "highly qualified teachers," as defined under the Elementary and Secondary Education Act (ESEA) of 1965, as amended, for the full five years of service.

Maximum benefit amount: Up to $5,000, in general, and up to $17,500 for special education teachers and secondary school teachers of mathematics or science. Forbearance from making loan payments may be granted during the five-year service period.

Restrictions on eligibility: Repayment benefits are available to borrowers who had no outstanding balance on any federal student loan made through a program authorized under Title IV of the HEA on October 1, 1998, or on the date the borrower first borrowed such a loan after October 1, 1998. Loans must have been obtained prior to the end of the five consecutive complete academic years of teaching service and may not be in default. Loan forgiveness may not be provided for the same service used to qualify for benefits under the Direct Loan Public Service Loan Forgiveness (PSLF) program, the Loan Forgiveness for Service in Areas of National Need program, or AmeriCorps education awards.

Post-award conditions: N/A

Federal tax treatment: The amount of student loans forgiven is excluded from gross income.

Budgetary classification and funding: Mandatory. Amounts provided for loan forgiveness are incorporated into student loan subsidy costs.

Amounts discharged or repaid: FY2009: $117.8 million. FY2010: $176.2 million. FY2011: $242.0 million. FY2012: $218.7 million. FY2013: $253.5 million.

Annual number of beneficiaries: FY2009: 14,514. FY2010: 20,791. FY2011: 28,975. FY2012: 27,358. FY2013: 31,262.

CRS report: CRS Report R40122, *Federal Student Loans Made Under the Federal Family Education Loan Program and the William D. Ford Federal Direct Loan Program: Terms and Conditions for Borrowers*, by David P. Smole.

Additional resources: U.S. Department of Education, Federal Student Aid, "Stafford Loan Forgiveness Program for Teachers," 2010.

Federal Perkins Loan Cancellation

Authority: Statute: HEA, Title IV, §465; 20 U.S.C. §1087ee. *Regulations:* 34 C.F.R. §674, Part D. *CFDA:* 84.037.

Federal administering agency: U.S. Department of Education, Federal Student Aid.

Purpose of program: To provide loan forgiveness benefits to borrowers of Perkins Loans for each complete year that they are employed or serve full-time in certain public service occupations.

Eligible loan types: Federal Perkins Loans.

Qualifying service or other activity: To qualify for cancellation benefits, borrowers must be employed or serve full-time in the following categories of occupations: teachers in low-income schools; staff in Head Start and other state-licensed preschool programs; special education teachers; members of the armed forces who serve in areas of hostilities; Peace Corps or AmeriCorps VISTA volunteers; law enforcement personnel and public defenders; teachers of mathematics, science, foreign languages, bilingual education, or other shortage subject areas; nurses and medical technicians; providers of social services to high-risk children; fire fighters; faculty members at Tribal Colleges and Universities; librarians with master's degrees in library science; and speech language pathologists who have a master's degree and who work exclusively with Elementary and Secondary Education Act, Title I-A schools.

Maximum benefit amount: Perkins Loan cancellation is based on both the number of years of service a borrower has completed and a rate of cancellation applicable to each particular type of service. For most types of service, up to 100% of a borrower's loan balance may be cancelled according to the following schedule: 15% of the outstanding loan balance is cancelled for each of the 1st and 2nd years of service; 20% is cancelled for each of the 3rd and 4th years of service; and the remaining 30% is cancelled for the 5th year of service. For service as Peace Corps and AmeriCorps VISTA volunteers, loan cancellation is provided at these rates for up to only four years of service (for a maximum of 70%). For work in Head Start and other state-licensed preschool programs, loan cancellation is provided at the rate of 15% per year for up to five years of service (for a maximum of 75%). Perkins Loan borrowers are also granted deferment from making payments on their loans (during which interest does not accrue) while performing service that qualifies for loan cancellation.

Restrictions on eligibility: Perkins Loans may not be cancelled for service performed prior to the loan being disbursed nor during the enrollment period covered by the loan. A complete year of service consists of 12 consecutive months of service, except for teaching service where a full academic year is considered a complete year of service. Loans to be repaid may not be in default. Loan forgiveness may not be provided for the same service used to qualify for AmeriCorps education awards.

Post-award conditions: N/A

Federal tax treatment: The amount of student loans cancelled is excluded from gross income

Budgetary classification and funding: The Secretary is required—to the extent feasible—to reimburse institutions of higher education for Perkins Loans that are cancelled for borrowers engaged in public service, however, funding for Perkins Loan cancellations is classified as discretionary for congressional budget purposes. Funds have not been appropriated for Perkins Loan cancellations since FY2009.

Amounts discharged or repaid: Information currently unavailable to CRS.

Annual number of beneficiaries: Information currently unavailable to CRS.

CRS report: CRS Report RL31618, *Campus-Based Student Financial Aid Programs Under the Higher Education Act*, by Alexandra Hegji and David P. Smole.

Additional resources: U.S. Department of Education, Federal Student Aid, 2012-2013 Federal Student Aid Handbook, Volume 6. Chapter 4—Perkins Repayment Plans Forbearance, Deferment, Cancellation, and Discharge, http://ifap.ed.gov/fsahandbook/attachments/ 1213FSAHbkVol6Ch4.pdf; and "Teacher Cancellation Low-Income Directory," https://www.tcli.ed.gov/CBSWebApp/tcli/.

Loan Forgiveness Following Income-Dependent Repayment Programs

Loan forgiveness following income-dependent repayment provides debt relief to borrowers who repay their federal student loans as a proportion of their income for an extended period of time but who have not repaid their entire student loan debt. These benefits are considered entitlements and are written into the terms and conditions of widely available federal student loans. They are potentially available to an open-ended number of qualified borrowers, but they are not intended to meet the traditional purpose of encouraging participation in specific occupations or service for which other federal loan forgiveness and repayment programs are intended.

Income-Contingent Repayment Plan A (ICR-A or Pay As You Earn Repayment Plan)

Authority: *Statute:* HEA, Title IV, §455(d)(1)(D) & (e); 20 U.S.C. §1087e(d)(1)(D) & (e). *Regulations:* 34 C.F.R. §§685.208(k) and 685.209. *CFDA:* 84.268.

Federal administering agency: U.S. Department of Education, Federal Student Aid.

Purpose of program: To provide certain borrowers of Direct Loan program loans the opportunity to make payment amounts that are determined according to a formula that establishes maximum payment amounts based on their Direct Loan program federal student loan debt, family size, and adjusted gross income (AGI), with any loan balance remaining after 20 years of ICR-A repayment being forgiven.

Eligible loan types: Direct Loan program Subsidized Loans, Unsubsidized Loans, Graduate PLUS Loans, and Consolidation Loans (other than Consolidation Loans used to repay Parent PLUS Loans), with any loan balance remaining after 20 years of ICR-A repayment being forgiven.

Qualifying service or other activity: To qualify for forgiveness benefits, borrowers must make payments towards their outstanding loans for the equivalent of 20 years. The 20-year repayment period that qualifies borrowers for loan forgiveness under the ICR-A plan includes periods during which payments were made according to the ICR-A plan; according to the ICR-B plan; according to the IBR plan, after no longer being eligible for or having left the IBR plan; or according to a standard repayment plan with a 10-year amortization and periods of economic hardship after October 1, 2007. Monthly payments are capped at 10% of a borrower's discretionary income.

Maximum benefit amount: There is no maximum benefit amount. Any loan balance that remains after 20 years of qualifying repayment is forgiven.

Restrictions on eligibility: Repayment according to the ICR-A plan is limited to individuals who had no outstanding loan balance on any DL or FFEL program loans on either October 1, 2007, or on the date they first borrowed after that date, and who on or after October 1, 2011 received a Direct Loan program loan disbursement or applied for and obtained a Direct Loan program Consolidation Loan. Eligibility to begin repaying according to the IBR-A plan is limited to borrowers whose student loan payments exceed 10% of their discretionary income. Borrowers may not be in default on their loans. During periods of repayment according to the ICR-A plan, the ICR-B plan, or the IBR plan, borrowers must annually provide the Secretary with documentation of their AGI (e.g., a copy of their federal tax return) and their family size.

Post-award conditions: N/A

Federal tax treatment: The amount of student loans forgiven is included in gross income, and borrowers are responsible for any tax obligation that results from the forgiveness of any student loan debt that remains after 20 years of repayment according to the ICR-A plan.

Budgetary classification and funding: Mandatory. Amounts provided for loan forgiveness are incorporated into student loan subsidy costs.

Amounts discharged or repaid: N/A. Borrowers have not yet been able to qualify for loan forgiveness by repaying loans according to the ICR-A plan for 20 years.

Annual Number of beneficiaries: N/A. Borrowers have not yet been able to qualify for loan forgiveness by repaying loans according to the ICR-A plan for 20 years.

CRS report: CRS Report R40122, *Federal Student Loans Made Under the Federal Family Education Loan Program and the William D. Ford Federal Direct Loan Program: Terms and Conditions for Borrowers*, by David P. Smole.

Additional resources: U.S. Department of Education, Federal Student Aid, "Income-Contingent Plan," http://studentaid.ed.gov/repay-loans/understand/plans/income-contingent. 77 *Federal Register* 212, November 1, 2012, pp. 66088-66147, http://www.gpo.gov/fdsys/pkg/FR-2012-11-01/pdf/2012-26348.pdf.

Income-Based Repayment (IBR) Plan for New Borrowers on or after July 1, 2014

Authority: *Statute:* HEA, Title IV, §493C; 20 U.S.C. §1098e. *Regulations:* 34 C.F.R. §682.215 and 685.221. *CFDA:* 84.032 and 84.268.

Federal administering agency: U.S. Department of Education, Federal Student Aid.

Purpose or description of program: The program will provide borrowers of Direct Loan program loans the opportunity to make payment amounts that are determined according to a formula that establishes maximum payment amounts based on their eligible federal student loan debt, family size, and adjusted gross income (AGI). Payments are capped at 10% of discretionary income. Any loan balance that remains after 20 years of IBR repayment will be forgiven.

Eligible loan types: Direct Loan program Subsidized Loans, Unsubsidized Loans, PLUS Loans made to graduate and professional students, and Consolidation Loans (except Consolidation Loans that repay a PLUS Loan made to a parent borrower).

Qualifying service or other activity: To qualify for repayment benefits, borrowers must make payments towards their outstanding loans for the equivalent of 20 years. The qualifying 20-year repayment period includes periods during which payments are made according to the IBR plan, the ICR-A plan, the ICR-B plan, a standard repayment plan with a 10-year amortization based on the loan amount at the time the borrower selected the IBR plan, or any repayment plan in amounts not less than the amount required according to a standard repayment plan with a 10-year amortization; and periods of economic hardship. Monthly payments are capped at 10% of a borrower's discretionary income.

Maximum benefit amount: There is no maximum benefit amount. Any loan balance that remains after 20 years of qualifying repayment will be forgiven.

Restrictions on eligibility: Borrowers may not be in default on their loans. During periods of repayment according to the IBR plan, the ICR-A plan, or the ICR-B plan, borrowers must annually provide the Secretary or their loan holder with documentation of their AGI (e.g., a copy of their federal tax return) and their family size.

Post-award conditions: N/A

Federal tax treatment: Recipients are responsible for any tax obligation that results from the forgiveness of any student loan debt that remains after 20 years of repayment according to the IBR plan.

Budgetary classification and funding: Mandatory. Amounts provided for IBR loan forgiveness are incorporated into student loan subsidy costs.

Amounts discharged or repaid: N/A. The program will only be available to individuals who have no outstanding balance of Direct Loan or FFEL program loans on July 1, 2014, or when they first borrow a Direct Loan program loan after July 1, 2014.

Annual number of beneficiaries: N/A. The program will only be available to individuals who have no outstanding balance of Direct Loan or FFEL program loans on July 1, 2014, or when they first borrow a Direct Loan program loan after July 1, 2014.

☐***R*☐ *report:*** CRS Report R40122, *Federal Student Loans Made Under the Federal Family Education Loan Program and the William D. Ford Federal Direct Loan Program: Terms and Conditions for Borrowers*, by David P. Smole.

Additional resources: U.S. Department of Education, Federal Student Aid, "Income-Based Plan," http://studentaid.ed.gov/repay-loans/understand/plans/income-based.

Income-Based Repayment (IBR) Plan for Pre-July 1, 2014, Borrowers

Authority: *Statute:* HEA, Title IV, §493C; 20 U.S.C. §1098e. *Regulations:* 34 C.F.R. §§682.215 and 685.221. *CFDA:* 84.032 and 84.268.

Federal administering agency: U.S. Department of Education, Federal Student Aid.

Purpose or description of program: To provide borrowers of Direct Loan and FFEL program loans the opportunity to make payment amounts that are determined according to a formula that establishes maximum payment amounts based on their eligible federal student loan debt, family size, and adjusted gross income (AGI), with any loan balance that remains after 25 years of IBR repayment being forgiven.

Eligible loan types: Direct Loan and FFEL program Subsidized Loans, Unsubsidized Loans, PLUS Loans made to graduate and professional students, and Consolidation Loans (except Consolidation Loans that repaid a Parent PLUS Loan).

Qualifying service or other activity: To qualify for forgiveness benefits, borrowers must make payments towards their outstanding loans for the equivalent of 25 years. The qualifying 25-year repayment period includes periods during which payments were made according to the IBR plan, the ICR-A plan, the ICR-B plan, a standard repayment plan with a 10-year amortization based on the loan amount at the time the borrower selected the IBR plan, or any repayment plan in amounts not less than the amount required according to a standard repayment plan with a 10-year amortization and periods of economic hardship. Monthly payments are capped at 15% of a borrower's discretionary income.

Maximum benefit amount: There is no maximum benefit amount. Any loan balance that remains after 25 years of qualifying repayment is forgiven.

Restrictions on eligibility: Borrowers may not be in default on their loans. During periods of repayment according to the IBR plan, the ICR-A plan, or the ICR-B plan, borrowers must annually provide the Secretary or their loan holder with documentation of their AGI (e.g., a copy of their federal tax return) and their family size.

Post-award conditions: N/A

Federal tax treatment: The amount of loans forgiven is included in gross income, and borrowers are responsible for any tax obligation that results from the forgiveness of any student loan debt that remains after 25 years of repayment according to the IBR plan.

Budgetary classification and funding: Mandatory. Amounts provided for IBR loan forgiveness are incorporated into student loan subsidy costs.

Amounts discharged or repaid: N/A. Borrowers have not yet been able to qualify for loan forgiveness by repaying loans according to the IBR plan for 25 years.

Annual number of beneficiaries: N/A. Borrowers have not yet been able to qualify for loan forgiveness by repaying loans according to the IBR plan for 25 years.

□*R*□ *report:* CRS Report R40122, *Federal Student Loans Made Under the Federal Family Education Loan Program and the William D. Ford Federal Direct Loan Program: Terms and Conditions for Borrowers*, by David P. Smole.

Additional resources: U.S. Department of Education, Federal Student Aid, "Income-Based Plan," http://studentaid.ed.gov/repay-loans/understand/plans/income-based.

Income-Contingent Repayment Plan B (ICR-B)

Authority: *Statute:* HEA, Title IV, §455(d)(1)(D) & (e); 20 U.S.C. §1087e(d)(1)(D) & (e). *Regulations:* 34 C.F.R. §685.208(k) and 685.209. *CFDA:* 84.268.

Federal administering agency: U.S. Department of Education, Federal Student Aid.

Purpose or description of program: To provide borrowers of Direct Loan program loans the opportunity to make payment amounts that are determined according to a formula that establishes maximum payment amounts based on their Direct Loan program federal student loan debt, family size, and adjusted gross income (AGI), with any loan balance remaining after 25 years of ICR-B repayment being forgiven.

Eligible loan types: Direct Loan program loans Subsidized Loans, Unsubsidized Loans, PLUS Loans, and Consolidation Loans (except PLUS Consolidation Loans). Consolidation Loans may include Direct Loan program PLUS Loans made to parent borrowers (if the loans were consolidated on or after July 1, 2006), and FFEL program loans.

Qualifying service or other activity: To qualify for forgiveness benefits, borrowers must make payments towards their outstanding loans for the equivalent of 25 years. The qualifying 25-year repayment period includes periods during which payments were made according to the ICR-B plan, the IBR plan, or standard repayment plans that have a 10-year amortization and periods of economic hardship after October 1, 2007. Monthly payments are generally capped at 20% of a borrower's discretionary income.

Maximum benefit amount: There is no maximum benefit amount. Any loan balance that remains after 25 years of qualifying repayment is forgiven.

Restrictions on eligibility: Borrowers may not be in default on their loans. During periods of repayment according to the ICR-A plan, the ICR-B plan, or the IBR plan, borrowers must annually provide the Secretary with documentation of their AGI (e.g., a copy of their federal tax return) and their family size.

Post-award conditions: N/A

Federal tax treatment: The amount of student loans forgiven is included in gross income, and borrowers are responsible for any tax obligation that results from the forgiveness of any student loan debt that remains after 25 years of repayment according to the ICR-B plan.

Budgetary classification and funding: Mandatory. Amounts provided for loan forgiveness are incorporated into student loan subsidy costs.

Amounts discharged or repaid: N/A. Borrowers have not yet been able to qualify for loan forgiveness by repaying loans according to the ICR-B plan for 25 years.

Annual number of beneficiaries: N/A. Borrowers have not yet been able to qualify for loan forgiveness by repaying loans according to the ICR-B plan for 25 years.

☐**R**☐ **report:** CRS Report R40122, *Federal Student Loans Made Under the Federal Family Education Loan Program and the William D. Ford Federal Direct Loan Program: Terms and Conditions for Borrowers*, by David P. Smole.

Additional Resources: U.S. Department of Education, Federal Student Aid, "Income-Contingent Plan," http://studentaid.ed.gov/repay-loans/understand/plans/income-contingent.

Loan Repayment for Public Service Employment Programs Supportive of Broad Employment Needs or Shortages

Loan repayment programs addressing broad employment needs or shortages are presented third in this appendix, as they are generally available to a limited number of qualified borrowers and subject to the appropriation of program funds, thus, they are likely to be smaller in scale than most, if not all, of the previously presented loan forgiveness programs.

Veterinary Medicine Loan Repayment Program

Authority: *Statute:* National Agricultural Research, Extension, and Teaching Policy Act of 1977, §1415A; 7 U.S.C. §3151a. *Regulations*: 7 C.F.R. §3431.1 et seq. *CFDA*: 10.313.

Federal administering agency: U.S. Department of Agriculture (USDA), National Institute of Food and Agriculture (NIFA).

Purpose of program: To provide loan repayment for large animal veterinarians who provide short-term services in designated shortage areas during emergency situations.

Eligible loan types: Any loan used to pay all or part of the cost of tuition and reasonable educational and living expenses to attend an accredited college of veterinary medicine, resulting in a Doctor of Veterinary Medicine or an equivalent (this may include FFEL and Direct Loan program Subsidized Loans, Unsubsidized Loans, PLUS Loans, and Consolidation Loans; Perkins Loans; and private education loans).

Qualifying service or other activity: To qualify for repayment benefits, borrowers must be large animal veterinarians who provide short-term services to the federal government in designated shortage areas during emergency situations. Borrowers must complete a maximum of 60 days of service per year for a minimum of three years and can agree to complete additional years of service.

Maximum benefit amount: $25,000 per year. Borrowers also receive salary and travel expenses during the time they are providing emergency services.

Restrictions on eligibility: Repayment benefits are awarded on a competitive basis, and borrowers must be nominated by State Animal Health Officials.

Post-award conditions: Individuals who breach their program contract are liable for an amount equal to the sum of: (1) the amount of loan repayments paid to the participant for a period of service not completed; (2) $7,500 multiplied by the months of service not completed; and (3) the interest on the sum of (1) and (2) calculated at the maximum prevailing rate—as determined by the Treasury—from the date of the contract breach.

Federal tax treatment: Borrowers can receive an additional 39% of the total loan repayment amount for income tax liability.

Budgetary classification and funding: Discretionary. Previous amounts appropriated, FY2009: $3.0 million. FY2010: $4.8 million. FY2011: $4.8 million. FY2012: $4.8 million. FY2013: $4.4 million.

Annual amounts discharged or repaid: FY2010: $5.19 million. FY2011: $7.25 million. FY2012: $4.5 million. FY2013: $3.8 million.

Annual number of beneficiaries: FY2010: 53. FY2011: 80. FY2012: 46. FY2013: 33 new awards and 10 award renewals. FY2013 was the first year in which renewal awards were made through the program.

☐***R***☐ ***reports:*** None.

Additional resources: U.S. Department of Agriculture, National Institute of Food and Agriculture, FY2010 Annual Report, http://www.nifa.usda.gov/nea/animals/in_focus/ an_health_if_vmlrp_repts_stats.html; U.S. Department of Agriculture, National Institute of Food and Agriculture, FY2011 Annual Report, http://www.nifa.usda.gov/nea/animals/in_focus/ an_health_if_vmlrp_repts_stats.html; USDA, NIFA Sample Veterinary Medicine Loan Repayment Program Contract, OMB No. 0524-0047, http://www.nifa.usda.gov/nea/animals/pdfs/ vmlrp_nifa_12_contract_sample.pdf; and U.S. Department of Agriculture, National Institute of Food and Agriculture, FY2013 Request for Applications, http://www.nifa.usda.gov/nea/animals/ pdfs/vmlrp_rfa_fy2013.pdf.

Indian Health Service Loan Repayment Program

Authority: Statute: Indian Health Care Improvement Act, Title I, §108; 25 U.S.C. §§1616a &1616a-1. *Regulations*: None. *CFDA:* 93.164.

Federal administering agency: U.S. Department of Health and Human Services (HHS), Indian Health Service (IHS).

Purpose of program: To assure an adequate supply of health professionals necessary to maintain accreditation of, and provide healthcare services to Indians through Indian health programs ("Indian health programs" refers to facilities operated by the IHS, an Indian Tribe, or a Tribal Organization).

Eligible loan types: Government and private loans obtained for tuition, other educational expenses, and reasonable living expenses for undergraduate education, graduate education, or both.

Qualifying service or other activity: To qualify for repayment benefits, borrowers must hold a degree in and be licensed in an eligible health profession, be enrolled in their final year of a health profession program at an accredited institution, or be enrolled in an approved graduate training program in a health profession. Eligible health professions are identified by the HHS Secretary. Borrowers must complete at least two years of service and can agree to complete additional years of service.

Maximum benefit amount: Up to $35,000 per year (generally, IHS makes annual awards of $20,000 per year).

Restrictions on eligibility: Repayment benefits are awarded on a competitive basis. Priority is given to American Indians and Alaska Natives, IHS scholarship recipients, current employees, certain health professions, and borrowers serving at the Indian Health Programs with the greatest shortages. Repayment benefits are limited to U.S. citizens or nationals. Borrowers must be eligible to hold an appointment as a commissioned officer in the Regular or Reserve Corps of the Public Health Service, be eligible for selection for a civilian service position in the Regular or Reserve Corps of the Public Health Service, and must meet the standards for civil service employment in the IHS or be employed in an Indian health program. Individuals may not have a service obligation under another program.

Post-award conditions: Borrowers must pay an amount equal to three times the loan repayments made on their behalf, plus interest, if they fail to complete their service commitment. The amount to be repaid is adjusted to account for any period of the service commitment that was completed.

Federal tax treatment: IHS makes additional payments, up to $4,000 per year, for any loan repayments that result in borrowers' income tax liability.

Budgetary classification and funding: Discretionary. The program is permanently authorized. Previous amounts appropriated include amounts appropriated for all IHS health professions programs. FY2009: $32.0 million. FY2010: $32.0 million. FY2011: $31.9 million. FY2013: $35.9 million. FY2013: $34.1 million.

Annual amounts discharged or repaid: FY2009: $17.2 million; FY2010: $19.2 million. FY2011: $20.9 million. FY2012: $21.3 million.

Annual number of beneficiaries: FY2009: 426 new awards and 197 contract extensions. FY2010: 338 new awards and 261 contract extensions. FY2011: 407 new awards and 294 contract extensions. FY2012: 504 new awards and 316 contract extensions. FY2013: 520 new awards and 290 contract extensions.

☐*R*☐ ***reports:*** CRS Report R41630, *The Indian Health Care Improvement Act Reauthorization and Extension as Enacted by the ACA: Detailed Summary and Timeline*, by Elayne J. Heisler; and CRS Report R43330, *The Indian Health Service (IHS): An Overview*, by Elayne J. Heisler.

Additional resources: U.S. Department of Health and Human Services, Indian Health Service, "IHS Loan Repayment Program Overview," http://www.ihs.gov/loanrepayment/; various years of the Department of Health and Human Services, Fiscal Year 2013 Indian Health Service, Justification of Estimates for Appropriations Committees.

National Health Service Corps Loan Repayment Program

Authority: *Statute:* PHSA, Title III, §§331-336, 338B-338E; 42 U.S.C. §§254d-254f, 254l-1, 254m, 254n, 254o. *Regulations:* 42 C.F.R. §62.21 et seq. *CFDA:* 93.162.

Federal administering agency: U.S. Department of Health and Human Services, Health Resources and Services Administration (HRSA).

Purpose of program: To eliminate health manpower shortages in health professional shortage areas (HPSAs).

Eligible loan types: Government and private loans obtained for tuition, other educational expenses, and reasonable living expenses for undergraduate education, graduate education, or both. PLUS loans made to parents are ineligible.

Qualifying service or other activity: To qualify for repayment benefits, borrowers must serve as a health professional in a HPSA as designated by HRSA. Borrowers must complete at least two years of service. Borrowers can enter into additional two-year service agreements.

Maximum benefit amount: Up to $60,000 per year or $240,000 in total. Loan repayment amounts vary by the HPSA score of the location where the borrowers are fulfilling their National Health Service Corps (NHSC) service commitment; borrowers serving at sites with lower HPSA scores (i.e., sites with less severe shortages) receive $40,000 per year. Clinicians may receive half of the typical amounts in return for half-time service (e.g., $30,000 or $20,000 per year in return for a two-year half-time commitment).

Restrictions on eligibility: Repayment benefits are awarded on a competitive basis, and awards may be based on the demonstrated interest of an applicant and other factors determined to be relevant. Repayment benefits are limited to U.S. citizens or nationals who are trained as, or in their last year of training to become, primary care physicians, dentists, primary care certified nurse practitioners, certified nurse midwives, primary care physician assistants, registered dental hygienists, health service psychologists, licensed clinical social workers, psychiatric nurse specialists, marriage and family therapists, or licensed professional counselors.

Post-award conditions: Borrowers must pay an amount equal to the sum of: (1) the amount of loan repayments paid to them for a period of service not completed; (2) $7,500 multiplied by the months of service not completed; and (3) the interest on the sum of (1) and (2) calculated at the maximum prevailing rate—as determined by the Treasury—from the date of the contract breach if they do not complete their service commitment.

Federal tax treatment: The amount of student loan repayments received is excluded from gross income if the loan meets certain conditions.

Budgetary classification and funding: Mandatory from FY2011 through FY2015 because of funds appropriated in the Affordable Care Act (P.L. 111-148, as amended) and discretionary thereafter. Previous amounts appropriated, FY2009: $63.4 million. FY2010: $77.7 million. ARRA: $156.1 million (ARRA funds were used for FY2010 and FY2011 loan repayments). FY2011: $197.4 million. FY2012: $161.2 million. FY2013: $169.7 million.

Annual amount discharged or repaid: Information currently unavailable to CRS.

Annual number of beneficiaries: FY2009: 949 new loan repayment awards and 705 continuations. FY2010: 1,335 new loan repayment awards and 701 continuations. ARRA: 3,267 new loan repayment awards. FY2011: 2,612 new loan repayment awards and 1,305 continuations. FY2012: 1,551 new loan repayment awards and 2,600 continuations. FY2013: 2,106 new loan repayment awards and 2,399 continuations.

☐***R*** ☐ ***reports:*** CRS Report R40181, *Selected Health Funding in the American Recovery and Reinvestment Act of 2009*, coordinated by C. Stephen Redhead; and CRS Report R41705, *The National Institutes of Health (NIH): Background and Congressional Issues*, by Judith A. Johnson.

Additional resources: Health Resources and Services Administration, *National Health Service Corps Loan Repayment Program Full-& Half-Time Service Opportunities: Fiscal Year 2013 Application and Program Guidance*, Rockville, MD, February 2013, http://nhsc.hrsa.gov/ downloads/lrpapplicationguidance.pdf; various years of the Department of Health and Human Services, Health Resources and Services Administration, Justification of Estimates for Appropriations Committees.

National Health Service Corps Students to Service Loan Repayment Program

Authority: Statute: PHSA, Title III, §§331-336, 338B-338E; 42 U.S.C. 254d-254f, 254l-1, 254m, 254n, 254o. *Regulations:* 42 C.F.R. §62.21 et seq. *CFDA:* 93.162.

Federal administering agency: U.S. Department of Health and Human Services, Health Resources and Services Administration.

Purpose of program: To eliminate health manpower shortages in health professional shortage areas (HPSAs).

Eligible loan types: Government and private loans obtained for tuition and other educational expenses and reasonable living expenses for undergraduate education, graduate education, or both. PLUS loans made to parents are ineligible.

Qualifying service or other activity: To qualify for repayment benefits, borrowers must practice full- or part-time primary care (internal medicine, family practice, pediatrics, obstetrics and gynecology, or geriatrics) at an approved site in a HPSA. Borrowers must complete three years of service.

Maximum benefit amount: Up to $30,000 per year or $120,000 total; a half-time option is available in exchange for a six-year service commitment.

Restrictions on eligibility: Repayment benefits are awarded on a competitive basis, and if there are more applicants than available funds, priority is given to applicants from disadvantaged backgrounds. Repayment benefits are available only to full-time medical students, who are U.S. citizens or U.S. nationals, in their last year of medical school. Borrowers must be planning to complete a residency in a primary care field (internal medicine, family practice, pediatrics, obstetrics and gynecology, or geriatrics).

Post-award conditions: Borrowers must pay an amount equal to the sum of: (1) the amount of loan repayments paid to them for a period of service not completed; (2) $7,500 multiplied by the months of service not completed; and (3) the interest on the sum of (1) and (2) calculated at the maximum prevailing rate—as determined by the Treasury—from the date of the contract breach if they do not complete their service commitment.

Federal tax treatment: The amount of student loan repayments received is excluded from gross income if the loan meets certain conditions.

Budgetary classification and funding: Mandatory from FY2011 through FY2015 because of funds appropriated in the Affordable Care Act (P.L. 111-148, as amended) and discretionary thereafter. Previous amounts appropriated, FY2012: $12 million. FY2013: $9.3 million.

Annual amounts discharged or repaid: Information currently unavailable to CRS.

Annual number of beneficiaries: The program began as a pilot program in FY2012, and 69 awards were made. FY2013: 78 new loan repayment awards made.

□R□ reports: None.

National Health Service Corps State Loan Repayment Program

Authority: *Statute:* PHSA, Title III, §338I; 42 U.S.C. §254q-1. *Regulations:* 42 C.F.R. §62.51 et seq. *CFDA:* 93.165.

Federal administering agency: U.S. Department of Health and Human Services, Health Resources and Services Administration.

Purpose of program: To increase the availability of primary care services in state-designated shortage areas.

Eligible loan types: Government and private loans obtained for tuition, other educational expenses, and reasonable living expenses for undergraduate education, graduate education, or both.

Qualifying service or other activity: To qualify for repayment benefits, borrowers must be health professionals who provide health services in a state-designated shortage area. Matching grants are provided to states operating National Health Service Corps student loan repayment programs (NHSCSLRPs). Service requirements and eligible health professions vary by state.

Maximum benefit amount: Amounts available vary by state. Amounts in excess of the amount provided to NHSC health professionals (NHSCLRP) must be awarded using state funds.

Restrictions on eligibility: Loan repayment awards criteria vary by state.

Post-award conditions: Borrowers must repay the relevant state if they do not complete their service commitment. States are required to have penalties in place for a breach; specific penalties vary by state.

Federal tax treatment: The amount of student loan repayments received is excluded from gross income if the loan meets certain conditions.

Budgetary classification and funding: Mandatory from FY2011 through FY2015 because of funds appropriated in the Affordable Care Act (P.L. 111-148, as amended) and discretionary thereafter. Previous amounts appropriated, FY2009: $10 million. ARRA: $10 million. FY2010: $10 million. FY2011: $10 million. FY2012: $9.4 million.

Annual amounts discharged or repaid: Information currently unavailable to CRS.

Annual number of beneficiaries: FY2009: 280. ARRA: 493 in FY2010 and FY2011. FY2010: 332. FY2011: 223. FY2012: 285. FY2013: 447.

□R□ reports: CRS Report R40181, *Selected Health Funding in the American Recovery and Reinvestment Act of 2009*, coordinated by C. Stephen Redhead.

Additional resources: NHSC, "State Loan Repayment," http://nhsc.hrsa.gov/loanrepayment/stateloanrepaymentprogram/index.html, and various years of the Department of Health and Human Services, Health Resources and Services Administration, Justification of Estimates for Appropriations Committees.

National Institutes of Health Extramural Loan Repayment Program: Health Disparities Research

Authority: *Statute:* PHSA, Title IV, §464z5; 42 U.S.C. §285t-2. *Regulations:* None. *CFDA:* 93.308.

Federal administering agency: U.S. Department of Health and Human Services, National Institutes of Health (NIH).

Purpose of program: To recruit highly qualified health professionals to conduct research on health disparities.

Eligible loan types: FFEL and Direct Loan program Subsidized Stafford Loans, Unsubsidized Stafford Loans, PLUS Loans (made after July 1, 2006), and Consolidation Loans; loans made available under PHSA Title VII-A and Title VIII-E; loans made or guaranteed by a state, the District of Columbia, the Commonwealth of Puerto Rico, or a territory or possession of the United States; loans made by academic institutions; and private education loans including MEDLOANS.

Qualifying service or other activity: To qualify for repayment benefits, borrowers must conduct research related to health disparities at an eligible institution (a domestic nonprofit foundation, a university, a professional association, another type of nonprofit institution, or a U.S. government agency (federal, state, or local)). Health disparities research is basic, clinical, or behavioral research on a health disparity population that includes the causes of health disparities and methods to diagnose and treat such disparities. Borrowers must hold a health professional degree (e.g., a doctoral degree in medicine, pharmacy, dentistry, optometry, osteopathic medicine, nursing, psychology, veterinary medicine) or a PhD. Borrowers must complete at least 20 hours of research per week for at least two years and can agree to complete one or two additional years of service.

Maximum benefit amount: Up to $35,000 per year.

Restrictions on eligibility: Repayment benefits are awarded on a competitive basis, based on NIH's research priorities. At least half of all loan repayment awards must go to individuals who are members of a health disparities population. Borrowers must be U.S. citizens or nationals and may not have a federal judgment or lien against their property. Borrowers must have qualifying educational debt in excess of 20% of their annual base salary. Borrowers must not have received support from any of the following programs: Physicians Shortage Area Scholarship Program, National Research Service Award Program, Public Health Service Scholarship Program, National Health Service Corps Scholarship Program, Primary Care Loan Program, Armed Forces (Army, Navy, or Air Force) Professions Scholarship Program, and the Indian Health Service Scholarship Program, but they may be eligible if they receive a deferral from their service commitment. Borrowers who breached another NIH loan repayment contract may not receive support under this program. Borrowers may not concurrently receive support under an NIH intramural research program or an NIH Cancer research and training program, and they may not receive any income from a for-profit source or from private practice.

Post-award conditions: Borrowers must pay $7,500 per month of service not completed, plus all the amounts paid on their behalf for the months that were not served. Borrowers must also pay for interest on the amount owed, with interest accruing from the date of breach. The U.S. government is entitled to recover not less than $31,000. Borrowers may terminate renewal contracts at any time without penalties. Loan repayments are prorated and terminated on the date that research stops.

Federal tax treatment: Borrowers can receive an additional 39% of the total loan repayment amount for federal income tax liability.

Budgetary classification and funding: Discretionary. Amounts appropriated are included in individual institute's operating budgets.

Annual amounts discharged or repaid: FY2009: $13.1 million. FY2010: $11.9 million. FY2011: $10.5 million. FY2012: $10.0 million.

Annual number of beneficiaries: FY2009: 168 new awards and 127 renewals. FY2010: 126 new awards and 136 renewals. FY2011: 122 new awards and 110 renewals. FY2012: 122 new awards and 120 renewals.

☐R☐ report: CRS Report R41705, *The National Institutes of Health (NIH): Background and Congressional Issues*, by Judith A. Johnson.

Additional resources: Various years of Department of Health and Human Services, National Institutes of Health, Justification of Estimates for Congressional Committees, Office of the Director, Washington, DC and U.S. Department of Health and Human Service, National Institutes of Health, NIH Division of Loan Repayment, Fiscal Year Highlights: The Extramural Loan Repayment Programs Data Book, Bethesda, MD, http://www.lrp.nih.gov/.

National Institutes of Health Extramural Loan Repayment Program: Contraception and Infertility Research

Authority: Statute: PHSA, Title IV, §487B; 42 U.S.C. §288-2. *Regulations*: 42 C.F.R. §68c. *CFDA:* 93.209.

Federal administering agency: U.S. Department of Health and Human Services, National Institutes of Health (NIH).

Purpose of program: To recruit highly qualified health professionals to conduct research at NIH on topics related to contraception and infertility.

Eligible loan types: FFEL and Direct Loan program Subsidized Loans, Unsubsidized Loans, PLUS Loans (made after July 1, 2006), and Consolidation Loans; loans made available under PHSA Title VII-A and Title VIII-E; loans made or guaranteed by a state, the District of Columbia, the Commonwealth of Puerto Rico, or a territory or possession of the United States; loans made by academic institutions; and private education loans including MEDLOANS.

Qualifying service or other activity: To qualify for repayment benefits, borrowers must conduct research on issues related to contraception and/or infertility at an eligible institution (a domestic nonprofit foundation, a university, a professional association, another type of nonprofit institution, or a U.S. government agency (federal, state, or local)). Borrowers must hold a health professional degree (e.g., a doctoral degree in medicine, pharmacy, dentistry, optometry, osteopathic medicine, nursing, psychology, veterinary medicine) or a PhD. Borrowers must complete at least 20 hours of research per week for at least two years and can agree to complete one or two additional years of service.

Maximum benefit amount: Up to $35,000 per year.

Restrictions on eligibility: Repayment benefits are awarded on a competitive basis, based on NIH's research priorities. Borrowers must be U.S. citizens or nationals and may not have a federal judgment or lien against their property. Individuals must have qualifying educational debt in excess of 20% of their annual base salary. Borrowers must not have received support from any of the following programs: Physicians Shortage Area Scholarship Program, National Research Service Award Program, Public Health Service Scholarship Program, National Health Service Corps Scholarship Program, Primary Care Loan Program, Armed Forces (Army, Navy, or Air Force) Professions Scholarship Program, and the Indian Health Service Scholarship Program, but they may be eligible if they receive a deferral from their service commitment. Borrowers who have breached another NIH loan repayment contract may not receive support under this program. Borrowers may not concurrently receive support under an NIH intramural research program or an NIH Cancer research and training program, and they may not receive any income from a for-profit source or from private practice.

Post-award conditions: Borrowers must pay $7,500 per month of service not completed, plus all the amounts paid on their behalf for months that were not served. Borrowers must also pay interest on the amount owed, with interest accruing from the date of breach. The U.S. government is entitled to recover not less than $31,000. Borrowers may terminate renewal contracts at any time without penalties. Loan repayments are prorated and terminated on the date that research stops.

Federal tax treatment: Borrowers can receive an additional 39% of the total loan repayment amount for federal income tax liability.

Budgetary classification and funding: Discretionary. Amounts appropriated are included in individual institute's operating budgets.

Annual amounts discharged or repaid: FY2009: $1.1 million. FY2010: $1.0 million. FY2011: $1.3 million. FY2012: $1.3 million.

Annual number of beneficiaries: FY2009: 15 new awards and 9 renewals. FY2010: 15 new awards and 8 renewals. FY2011: 19 new awards and 11 renewals. FY2012: 19 new awards and 11 renewals.

☐*R*☐ *report:* CRS Report R41705, *The National Institutes of Health (NIH): Background and Congressional Issues*, by Judith A. Johnson.

Additional resources: Various years of Department of Health and Human Services, National Institutes of Health, Justification of Estimates for Congressional Committees, Office of the Director, Washington, DC and U.S. Department of Health and Human Service, National Institutes of Health, NIH Division of Loan Repayment, Fiscal Year Highlights: The Extramural Loan Repayment Programs Data Book, Bethesda, MD, http://www.lrp.nih.gov/.

National Institutes of Health Extramural Loan Repayment Program: Clinical Research

Authority: Statute: PHSA, Title IV, §487F; 42 U.S.C. §288-5a. *Regulations*: None. *CFDA:* 93.280.

Federal administering agency: U.S. Department of Health and Human Services, National Institutes of Health (NIH).

Purpose of program: To recruit highly qualified health professionals to conduct clinical research.

Eligible loan types: FFEL and Direct Loan program Subsidized Loans, Unsubsidized Loans, PLUS Loans (made after July 1, 2006), and Consolidation Loans; loans made available under PHSA Title VII-A and Title VIII-E; loans made or guaranteed by a state, the District of Columbia, the Commonwealth of Puerto Rico, or a territory or possession of the United States; loans made by academic institutions; and private education loans including MEDLOANS.

Qualifying service or other activity: To qualify for repayment benefits, borrowers must conduct research at an eligible institution (a domestic nonprofit foundation, a university, a professional association, another type of nonprofit institution, or a U.S. government agency (federal, state, or local)). Borrowers must hold a health professional degree (e.g., a doctoral degree in medicine, pharmacy, dentistry, optometry, osteopathic medicine, nursing, psychology, veterinary medicine) or a PhD. Borrowers must complete at least 20 hours of research per week for at least two years and can agree to complete one or two additional years of service.

Maximum benefit amount: Up to $35,000 per year.

Restrictions on eligibility: Repayment benefits are awarded on a competitive basis, based on NIH's research priorities. Borrowers must be U.S. citizens or nationals and may not have a federal judgment or lien against their property. Borrowers must have qualifying educational debt in excess of 20% of their annual base salary. Borrowers must not have received support from any of the following programs: Physicians Shortage Area Scholarship Program, National Research Service Award Program, Public Health Service Scholarship Program, National Health Service Corps Scholarship Program, Primary Care Loan Program, Armed Forces (Army, Navy, or Air Force) Professions Scholarship Program, and the Indian Health Service Scholarship Program, but they may be eligible if they receive a deferral from their service commitment. Borrowers who breached another NIH loan repayment contract may not receive support under this program. Borrowers may not concurrently receive support under an NIH intramural research program or an NIH Cancer research and training program, and they may not receive any income from a for-profit source or from private practice.

Post-award conditions: Borrowers must pay $7,500 per month of service not completed, plus all the amounts paid on their behalf for months that were not served. Borrowers must also pay interest on the amount owed, with interest accruing from the date of breach. The U.S. government is entitled to recover not less than $31,000. Borrowers may terminate renewal contracts at any time without penalties. Loan repayments are prorated and terminated on the date that research stops.

Federal tax treatment: Borrowers can receive an additional 39% of the total loan repayment amount for federal income tax liability.

Budgetary classification and funding: Discretionary. Amounts appropriated are included in individual institute's operating budgets.

Annual amounts discharged or repaid: FY2009: $40.2 million. FY2010: $44.9 million. FY2011: $40.5 million. FY2012: $39.6 million.

Annual number of beneficiaries: FY2009: 410 new awards and 469 renewals. FY2010: 464 new awards and 470 renewals. FY2011: 404 new awards and 468 renewals. FY2012: 389 new awards and 493 renewals.

R report: CRS Report R41705, *The National Institutes of Health (NIH): Background and Congressional Issues*, by Judith A. Johnson.

Additional resources: Various years of Department of Health and Human Services, National Institutes of Health, Justification of Estimates for Congressional Committees, Office of the Director, Washington, DC and U.S. Department of Health and Human Service, National Institutes of Health, NIH Division of Loan Repayment, Fiscal Year Highlights: The Extramural Loan Repayment Programs Data Book, Bethesda, MD, http://www.lrp.nih.gov/.

National Institutes of Health Extramural Loan Repayment Program: Pediatric Research

Authority: *Statute:* PHSA, Title IV, §487F; 42 U.S.C. §288-6. *Regulations*: None. *CFDA:* 93.285.

Federal administering agency: U.S. Department of Health and Human Services, National Institutes of Health (NIH).

Purpose of program: To recruit highly qualified health professionals to conduct pediatric research.

Eligible loan types: FFEL and Direct Loan program Subsidized Loans, Unsubsidized Loans, PLUS Loans (made after July 1, 2006), and Consolidation Loans; loans made available under PHSA Title VII-A and Title VIII-E; loans made or guaranteed by a state, the District of Columbia, the Commonwealth of Puerto Rico, or a territory or possession of the United States; loans made by academic institutions; and private education loans including MEDLOANS.

Qualifying service or other activity: To qualify for repayment benefits, borrowers must conduct research on issues related to children's health at an eligible institution (a domestic nonprofit foundation, a university, a professional association, another type of nonprofit institution, or a U.S. government agency (federal, state, or local)). Borrowers must complete at least 20 hours of research per week for at least two years and can agree to complete one or two additional years of service.

Maximum benefit amount: Up to $35,000 per year.

Restrictions on eligibility: Repayment benefits are awarded on a competitive basis, based on NIH's research priorities. Borrowers must be U.S. citizens or nationals and may not have a federal judgment or lien against their property. Borrowers must have qualifying educational debt in excess of 20% of their annual base salary. Borrowers must not have received support from any of the following programs: Physicians Shortage Area Scholarship Program, National Research Service Award Program, Public Health Service Scholarship Program, National Health Service Corps Scholarship Program, Primary Care Loan Program, Armed Forces (Army, Navy, or Air Force) Professions Scholarship Program, and the Indian Health Service Scholarship Program, but they may be eligible if they receive a deferral from their service commitment. Borrowers who breached another NIH loan repayment contract may not receive support under this program. Borrowers may not concurrently receive support under an NIH intramural research program or an NIH Cancer research and training program, and they may not receive any income from a for-profit source or from private practice.

Post-award conditions: Borrowers must pay $7,500 per month of service not completed, plus all the amounts paid on their behalf for months that were not served. Borrowers must also pay interest on the amount owed, with interest accruing from the date of breach. The U.S. government is entitled to recover not less than $31,000. Borrowers may terminate renewal contracts at any time without penalties. Loan repayments are prorated and terminated on the date that research stops.

Federal tax treatment: Borrowers can receive an additional 39% of the total loan repayment amount for federal income tax liability.

Budgetary classification and funding: Discretionary. Amounts appropriated are included in individual institute's operating budgets.

Annual amounts discharged or repaid: FY2009: $18.2 million. FY2010: $16.3 million. FY2011: $18.4 million. FY2012: $19.0 million.

Annual number of beneficiaries: FY2009: 175 new awards and 213 renewals. FY2010: 159 new awards and 176 renewals. FY2011: 185 new awards and 227 renewals. FY2012: 168 new awards and 214 renewals.

☐*R*☐ *report:* CRS Report R41705, *The National Institutes of Health (NIH): Background and Congressional Issues*, by Judith A. Johnson.

Additional resources: Various years of Department of Health and Human Services, National Institutes of Health, Justification of Estimates for Congressional Committees, Office of the Director, Washington, DC and U.S. Department of Health and Human Service, National Institutes of Health, NIH Division of Loan Repayment, Fiscal Year Highlights: The Extramural Loan Repayment Programs Data Book, Bethesda, MD, http://www.lrp.nih.gov/.

Loan Repayments for Health Professional School Faculty

Authority: Statute: PHSA, Title VII, §738(a); 42 U.S.C. §293b. *Regulations:* None. *CFDA:* 93.923.

Federal administering agency: U.S. Department of Health and Human Services, Health Resources and Services Administration.

Purpose of program: To provide loan repayment benefits to borrowers from disadvantaged backgrounds, based on environmental and/or economic factors, and who serve as faculty at health professions schools.

Eligible loan types: Government and private loans obtained for tuition, other educational expenses, and reasonable living expenses for undergraduate education, graduate education, or both.

Qualifying service or other activity: To qualify for loan repayment, borrowers must be from a disadvantaged background—based on environmental and/or economic factors—have a degree in medicine, osteopathic medicine, dentistry, nursing, or another health profession or be in the final year of study in an approved graduate training program in one of these fields and agree to serve as faculty at a school of medicine, nursing, osteopathic medicine, pharmacy, allied health, podiatric medicine, optometry, veterinary medicine, or public health, or at a school offering physician assistant education programs or graduate programs in behavioral and mental health. Borrowers must complete at least two years of service.

Maximum benefit amount: Up to $40,000 for a two-year period or $20,000 per year.

Restrictions on eligibility: Repayment benefits are awarded on a competitive basis. Borrowers must be U.S. citizens or nationals from disadvantaged backgrounds, based on environmental and/or economic factors.

Post-award conditions: Borrowers are placed in default and are liable for an amount equal to the sum of the amount of loan repayments paid to them for a period of service not completed, plus 39% of that amount (representing the amount paid/withheld for federal taxes on that amount), and $1,000 for each month of service not completed if borrowers do not complete their service commitment. Borrowers breaching their service contract are ineligible to apply for this program in the future and may also be disqualified from certain other federal programs.

Federal tax treatment: Borrowers receive funds, up to 39% of the award amount, to offset the tax burden associated with receiving loan repayment.

Budgetary classification and funding: Discretionary. Previous amounts appropriated, FY2009: $1.27 million. ARRA: $1.2 million. FY2010: $1.27 million. FY2011: $1.26 million. FY2012: $1.24 million. FY2013: $1.08 million.

Annual amounts discharged or repaid: Information currently unavailable to CRS.

Annual number of beneficiaries: FY2009: 23. ARRA: 22. FY2010: 23. FY2011: 20. FY2012: 20. FY2013: 21.

☐*R*☐*reports:* CRS Report R41278, *Public Health, Workforce, Quality, and Related Provisions in ACA: Summary and Timeline*, coordinated by C. Stephen Redhead and Elayne J. Heisler; CRS Report R43177, *Health Workforce Programs in Title VII of the Public Health Service Act*, by Bernice Reyes-Akinbileje; and CRS Report R40181, *Selected Health Funding in the American Recovery and Reinvestment Act of 2009*, coordinated by C. Stephen Redhead.

Additional resources: U.S. Department of Health and Human Services, Health Resources and Services Administration, "Faculty Loan Repayment Program," http://www.hrsa.gov/ loanscholarships/repayment/Faculty/index.html; Department of Health and Human Services: American Recovery and Reinvestment Act: Improving and Preserving Health Care, Health Resources and Services Administration: Health Professions Programs, Washington, DC, June 2010, http://www.hhs.gov/recovery/reports/plans/pdf20100610/ HRSA%20Health%20Professions%20Training%20%20June%202010.pdf; and various years of the Department of Health and Human Services, Health Resources and Services Administration, Justification of Estimates for Appropriations Committees.

General, Pediatric, and Public Health Dentistry Faculty Loan Repayment

Authority: Statute: PHSA, Title VII, §748(a)(2); 42 U.S.C. §293k-2. *Regulations:* None. *CFDA:* 93.059.

Federal administering agency: U.S. Department of Health and Human Services, Health Resources and Services Administration.

Purpose of program: To provide loan repayment for general, pediatric, and public health dental faculty.

Eligible loan types: Any outstanding student loan (this may include FFEL and Direct Loan program Subsidized Loans, Unsubsidized Loans, PLUS Loans, and Consolidation Loans; Perkins Loans; and private education loans).

Qualifying service or other activity: Borrowers must serve as full-time faculty in general, pediatric, or public health dentistry.

Maximum benefit amount: Borrowers receive the following loan repayment amounts for each year of service as a full-time faculty member: 10% of their student loan balance in the first year, 15% in the second year, 20% in the third year, 25% in the fourth year, and 30% in the fifth year.

Restrictions on eligibility: Grants are awarded on a competitive basis to dental or dental hygiene schools or approved residency or advanced education programs in general, pediatric, or public health dentistry to, among other activities, award repayment benefits. Entities may partner with schools of public health.

Post-award conditions: N/A

Federal tax treatment: N/A

Budgetary classification and classification: Discretionary. Previous amounts appropriated FY2009: $20 million. FY2010: $15 million;. FY2011: $15 million. FY2012: $20 million. FY2013:$20 million. This amount is the entire appropriation for all training in general, pediatric, and public health dentistry programs; amount includes, but is not exclusive to, loan repayment.

Annual amounts discharged or repaid: Information currently unavailable to CRS.

Annual number of beneficiaries: FY2009: N/A. FY2010: 18. FY2011: 28. FY2012: 35. FY2013: 28.

☐R☐ reports: CRS Report R41278, *Public Health, Workforce, Quality, and Related Provisions in ACA: Summary and Timeline*, coordinated by C. Stephen Redhead and Elayne J. Heisler; and CRS Report R43177, *Health Workforce Programs in Title VII of the Public Health Service Act*, by Bernice Reyes-Akinbileje.

Additional resources: None.

Nursing Education Loan Repayment Program (NURSE Corps)

Authority: Statute: PHSA Title VIII, §846(a), (b), & (c); 42 U.S.C. §297n & 297n-1. *Regulations:* 42 C.F.R. §57.312. *CFDA:* 93.908.

Federal administering agency: U.S. Department of Health and Human Services, Health Resources and Services Administration.

Purpose of program: To provide loan repayment benefits to borrowers who serve as nurses at healthcare facilities with a critical shortage of nurses or as nurse faculty at accredited schools of nursing.

Eligible loan types: Eligible loans include those made under nursing student loan programs and any other education loan for nurse training costs (relevant loan programs are not specified).

Qualifying service or other activity: To qualify for repayment benefits, borrowers must serve as nurses at nonprofit healthcare facilities with a shortage of nurses or as nurse faculty at accredited schools of nursing. Nurses at shortage facilities must have received a diploma or a baccalaureate, associate, or graduate degree in nursing in exchange for services as a nurse at a nonprofit healthcare facility. Nurse faculty members must have received a graduate degree. Borrowers must complete at least two years of service.

Maximum benefit amount: Up to 85% of a borrower's loan balance may be repaid in the following installments: 30% of the principal and interest of their loan balance in exchange for one year of service; another 30% of the principal and interest in exchange for the second year of service; and 25% in exchange for a third year of service.

Restrictions on eligibility: Repayment benefits are awarded on a competitive basis. Funding preference is giving to: (1) applicants with the greatest financial need, defined as individuals whose loans are 20% or greater of their annual base salary and (2) individuals who either work in facilities that have the most severe nursing shortages or as nursing faculty. Awards are made first to applicants who meet the debt-to-income ratio criteria. Within this category, individuals employed at facilities that target the underserved and faculty members at nursing schools receive preference.

Post-award conditions: Borrowers must repay the amount of all student loan payments received, plus interest, at the maximum legal prevailing rate from the date of breach if they do not complete their service commitment. Borrowers who breach a one-year continuation contract are liable to repay all loan repayments received for the third year of service (including amounts withheld for federal taxes), plus interest, at the maximum legal prevailing rate from the date of breach. Borrowers who breach either an initial or continuing loan repayment award are also permanently disqualified from receiving future awards under this or another federal loan repayment program. Borrowers who breach a loan repayment award must repay the amount owed to the federal government (including interest amount owed) within three years of the breach date. Borrowers who do not repay within the three year period may be assessed penalties.

Federal tax treatment: The amount of student loan repayments received is included in gross income.

Budgetary classification and funding: Discretionary. Amounts provided are subject to annual appropriations through FY2014. Previous amounts appropriated, FY2009: $22.8 million. ARRA: $27 million for both program scholarships and loan repayments. FY2010: $57.0 million. FY2011: $57.5 million. FY2012: $50.9 million. FY2013: $78.0 million for both program scholarships and loan repayments.

Annual amounts discharged or repaid: Information currently unavailable to CRS.

Annual number of beneficiaries: FY2009: 392 new loan repayment awards and 171 award extensions. ARRA: 427 new loan repayment awards. FY2010: 1139 new loan repayment awards and 135 award extensions. FY2011: 919 new loan repayment awards and 385 award extensions. FY2012: 720 new loan repayment awards and 732 award extensions. FY2013: 580 new loan repayment awards and 606 award extensions.

□*R*□ ***reports:*** CRS Report R41737, *Public Health Service (PHS) Agencies: Overview and Funding, FY2010-FY2012*, coordinated by C. Stephen Redhead and Pamela W. Smith; and CRS Report R40181, *Selected Health Funding in the American Recovery and Reinvestment Act of 2009*, coordinated by C. Stephen Redhead.

Additional resources: U.S. Department of Health and Human Services, Health Resources and Services Administration, "Nursing Education Loan Repayment Program Overview," http://www.hrsa.gov/loanscholarships/repayment/nursing/fundingpreference.html; U.S. Department of Health and Human Services, Health Resources and Services Administration, " Loan Repayment Program, NURSE Corps," http://www.hrsa.gov/loanscholarships/repayment/nursing/index.html; and various years of the Department of Health and Human Services, Health Resources and Services Administration, Justification of Estimates for Appropriations Committees.

Nursing Faculty Loan Repayment Program

Authority: Statute: PHSA Title VIII, §846A; 42 U.S.C. §297n-1. *Regulations*: None. *CFDA:* 93.264.

Federal administering agency: U.S. Department of Health and Human Services, Health Resources and Services Administration.

Purpose of program: To increase the number of qualified nursing faculty.

Eligible loan types: Government and private loans obtained for tuition, fees, books, other educational expenses, and reasonable living expenses. Eligible loans must be repayable over a 10-year period that begins 9 months after a borrower completes nursing school, and the interest rate is limited to 3% per year. Individual nursing schools operating a loan repayment fund may determine eligible loan types that meet the above criteria.

Qualifying service or other activity: To qualify for repayment benefits, borrowers must serve as full-time faculty at accredited nursing schools.

Maximum benefit amount: Up to 85% of a borrower's loan balance may be repaid in the following installments: 20% of their loan balance for each of three years of service and 25% of their loan balance for a fourth year of service. In FY2010 and FY2011, amounts repaid in a given year could not exceed $35,500; this limit is adjusted annually to reflect cost of attendance increases.

Restrictions on eligibility: Grants are awarded on a competitive basis to nursing schools to establish a loan repayment program. Individual nursing schools determine repayment recipients.

Post-award conditions: N/A

Federal tax treatment: The amount of student loan repayments received is included in gross income.

Budgetary classification and funding: Discretionary. Amounts provided are subject to annual appropriations through FY2014. Previous amounts appropriated, FY2009: $11.5 million. ARRA: $12 million. FY2010: $24.9 million. FY2011: $24.8 million. FY2012: $24.5 million. FY2013: $23.3 million. These amounts represent the amounts awarded to schools to administer student loan funds and not the amounts used for loan repayment.

Annual amounts discharged or repaid: Information currently unavailable to CRS.

Annual number of beneficiaries: Information currently unavailable to CRS.

R reports: CRS Report R43304, *Public Health Service Agencies: Overview and Funding*, coordinated by C. Stephen Redhead; and CRS Report R41278, *Public Health, Workforce, Quality, and Related Provisions in ACA: Summary and Timeline*, coordinated by C. Stephen Redhead and Elayne J. Heisler.

Additional resources: U.S. Department of Health and Human Services, Health Resources and Services Administration, "Nurse Faculty Loan Program (NFLP)," http://bhpr.hrsa.gov/nursing/

grants/nflp.html and various years of the Department of Health and Human Services, Health Resources and Services Administration, Justification of Estimates for Appropriations Committees.

John R. Justice (JRJ) Loan Repayment for Prosecutors and Public Defenders Program

Authority: *Statute:* The Omnibus Crime Control and Safe Streets Act of 1968, as amended, Title I, Part JJ, §3001; 42 U.S.C. §3797cc-21. *Regulations:* None. *CFDA:* 16.816.

Federal administering agency: U.S. Department of Justice, Bureau of Justice Assistance.

Purpose or description of program: To encourage qualified attorneys to enter and continue employment as prosecutors and public defenders.

Eligible loan types: FFEL and Direct Loan program Subsidized Loans, Unsubsidized Loans, Graduate PLUS Loans, and Consolidation Loans (other than Consolidation Loans used to repay Parent PLUS Loans); and Perkins Loans.

Qualifying service or other activity: To qualify for repayment benefits, borrowers must be employed as full-time prosecutors, public defenders, or federal defender attorneys. Borrowers must be attorneys who are continually licensed to practice law and must complete at least three years of service.

Maximum benefit amount: Up to $10,000 per year and $60,000 in cumulative benefits.

Restrictions on eligibility: Borrowers may not be in default on their loans. The program is administered as a partnership between the Bureau of Justice Assistance and state governors. Funds are awarded to states to operate loan repayment programs. In general, within each state, loan repayment benefits must be equally distributed between prosecutors and public defenders. Within each state, priority consideration must be given to eligible beneficiaries who have the least ability to repay their student loans. While receiving loan repayment benefits, recipients are required to continue making payments on their federal student loans. Individuals who receive benefits in one year are not guaranteed to receive benefits for any subsequent years that are covered by a service agreement. Funds for loan repayment are allocated to states in proportion to each state's share of the national population, with a minimum state allocation of $100,000.

Post-award conditions: Borrowers must notify the state agency that administers the program if they transfer to a new position or employer, if they intend to voluntarily leave their position, or if they default on their loans. Borrowers must repay the Department of Justice for any benefits received if, prior to completing the required three-year term of service, they voluntarily separate from employment or are involuntarily separated for misconduct or unacceptable performance.

Federal tax treatment: The amount of student loans repaid is excluded from gross income.

Budgetary classification and funding: Discretionary. Amounts provided are subject to annual appropriations for FY2010 through FY2015. Previous amount appropriated, FY2009: $25 million. FY2010: $10 million. FY2011: $8.2 million. FY2012: $4 million. FY2013: $3.71 million.

Amounts discharged or repaid: Information currently unavailable to CRS.

Annual number of beneficiaries: States (including the District of Columbia and U.S. territories) receiving grants to make awards, FY2010: 51. FY2011: 56. FY2012: 56. FY2013: 55.

☐*R*☐ *reports:* None.

Additional resources: U.S. Department of Justice, Bureau of Justice Assistance, "John R. Justice (JRJ) Program," https://www.bja.gov/ProgramDetails.aspx?Program_ID=65; "John R. Justice (JRJ) Grant Program, FY2014 State Solicitation Frequently Asked Questions (FAQs) (Revised 12/24/2013)," https://www.bja.gov/Funding/14JRJFAQ.pdf. Letter from U.S. Department of the Treasury, Internal Revenue Service to Rafael A. Madan, General Counsel, Department of Justice, December 31, 2012, https://www.bja.gov/Programs/IRS-JRJ-Letter.pdf. U.S. Department of Justice, Office of the Inspector General, Audit of the Office of Justice Programs Bureau of Justice Assistance John R. Justice Grant Program, Audit Report 14-23, May 2014, http://www.justice.gov/oig/reports/2014/a1423.pdf.

Civil Legal Assistance Attorney Student Loan Repayment Program

Authority: Statute: HEA, Title IV, §428L; 20 U.S.C. §1078-12. *Regulations:* None. *CFDA:* 84.409.

Federal administering agency: U.S. Department of Education, Federal Student Aid.

Purpose of program: To encourage qualified individuals to enter into and continue employment as civil legal assistance attorneys.

Eligible loan types: FFEL and Direct Loan program Subsidized Loans, Unsubsidized Loans, Graduate PLUS Loans, and Consolidation Loans (other than Consolidation Loans used to repay Parent PLUS Loans) and Perkins Loans.

Qualifying service or other activity: To qualify for repayment benefits, borrowers must enter into service agreements to remain employed full-time as civil legal assistance attorneys and must be continually licensed to practice law. Borrowers must complete at least three years of service, and they subsequently can agree to complete additional year of service.

Maximum benefit amount: Up to $6,000 per year and $40,000 cumulatively.

Restrictions on eligibility: Loan repayment benefits are made available to borrowers on a first-come, first-served basis and are subject to the appropriation of funds for each fiscal year. Benefits are only available until funds are fully committed and the receipt of benefits in one year does not guarantee benefits for subsequent years covered by a service agreement. Loans to be repaid may not be in default. Loan forgiveness may not be provided for the same service used to qualify for benefits under the Loan Forgiveness for Service in Areas of National Need program or the Direct Loan Public Service Loan Forgiveness (PSLF) program.

Post-award conditions: Borrowers must repay any benefits received if they voluntarily separate from employment or are involuntarily separated for misconduct before the end of the service agreement.

Federal tax treatment: The amount of student loans repaid is excluded from gross income.

Budgetary classification and funding: Discretionary. Amounts provided are subject to annual appropriations for FY2010 through FY2014. Previous amounts appropriated, FY2009: $10 million. FY2010: $5 million. No appropriations were provided for FY2011 through FY2014.

Amounts discharged or repaid: Information currently unavailable to CRS.

Annual number of beneficiaries: Information currently unavailable to CRS.

☐R☐ reports: None.

Additional resources: U.S. Department of Education, Federal Student Aid, "Civil Legal Assistance Attorney Student Loan Repayment Program Questions and Answers," July 1, 2010, http://studentaid.ed.gov/sites/default/files/claarp-fact-sheet.pdf.

Public Health Workforce Loan Repayment Program

Authority: Statute: PHSA §776; 42 U.S.C. §295f-1. *Regulations*: None. *CFDA:* None.

Federal administering agency: U.S. Department of Health and Human Services (HHS), Health Resources and Services Administration.

Purpose of program: To assure an adequate supply of public health professionals to eliminate critical public health workforce shortages in federal, state, local, and tribal public health agencies.

Eligible loan types: Any loan used to pay for the borrower's undergraduate or graduate education (this may include FFEL and Direct Loan program Subsidized Loans, Unsubsidized Loans, PLUS Loans, and Consolidation Loans; Perkins Loans; and private education loans).

Qualifying service or other activity: To qualify for repayment benefits, borrowers must be employed full-time or have accepted a full-time position at a federal, state, local, or tribal public health agency or must be completing a related training fellowship. Borrowers must complete at least three years of service in a priority service area as determined by the HHS Secretary.

Maximum benefit amount: $35,000 per year for borrowers with a student loan balance greater than $105,000 and one-third of the loan balance per year for borrowers with a lower balance.

Restrictions on eligibility: Repayment benefits are awarded on a competitive basis. Borrowers must be U.S. citizens and must not have received benefits under the Public Service Loan Forgiveness, Stafford Loan Forgiveness for Teachers, Loan Forgiveness for Service in Areas of National Need, Civil Legal Assistance Attorneys Loan Repayment, or Perkins Loan Cancellation programs for the same service. Borrowers must have graduated in the last 10 years with a public health or health professions degree.

Post-award conditions: Borrowers must pay an amount equal to the sum of: (1) the amount of loan repayments paid to them for a period of service not completed; (2) $7,500 multiplied by the months of service not completed; and (3) the interest on the sum of (1) and (2) calculated at the maximum prevailing rate—as determined by the Treasury—from the date of the contract breach if they do not complete their service commitment.

Federal tax treatment: Borrowers can receive an additional 39% of the total loan repayment amount for income tax liability.

Budgetary classification and funding: Discretionary. Funding was last appropriated in FY2010.

Annual amounts discharged or repaid: N/A

Annual number of beneficiaries: N/A

◻R◻ reports: CRS Report R41278, *Public Health, Workforce, Quality, and Related Provisions in ACA: Summary and Timeline,* coordinated by C. Stephen Redhead and Elayne J. Heisler; and CRS Report R43177, *Health Workforce Programs in Title VII of the Public Health Service Act,* by Bernice Reyes-Akinbileje.

Additional resources: None.

Loan Forgiveness for Service in Areas of National Need

Authority: Statute: HEA, Title IV, §428K; 20 U.S.C. §1078-11. *Regulations:* None. *CFDA:* None.

Federal administering agency: U.S. Department of Education.

Purpose or description of program: To provide loan forgiveness to borrowers who are employed full-time in an area of national need.

Eligible loan types: FFEL and Direct Loan program Subsidized Loans, Unsubsidized Loans, Graduate PLUS Loans, and Consolidation Loans (other than Consolidation Loans used to repay Parent PLUS Loans).

Qualifying service or other activity: To qualify for forgiveness benefits, borrowers must be employed full-time in one of the following areas of national need: early childhood educator; nurse; foreign language specialist; librarian; highly qualified teacher; child welfare worker; speech-language pathologist or audiologist; school counselor; public sector employee in public safety, emergency management, public health, or public interest legal services; nutrition professional; medical specialist; mental health professional; dentist; employee in the science, technology, engineering, and mathematics (STEM) fields; physical therapist; superintendent, principal, or other (school) administrator; occupational therapist; and allied health professional.

Maximum benefit amount: Up to $2,000 per school year, academic year, or calendar year of full-time employment in an area of national need completed on or after August 14, 2008 and $10,000 cumulatively.

Restrictions on eligibility: Forgiveness benefits are available to borrowers on a first-come, first-served basis. Full-time employment in an area of national need must be completed on or after August 14, 2008, and loans to be forgiven may not be in default. Loan forgiveness may not be provided for the same service used to qualify for benefits under the Stafford Loan Forgiveness for Teachers program, the Direct Loan Public Service Loan Forgiveness (PSLF) program, or the Civil Legal Assistance Attorney Student Loan Repayment Program (CLAARP).

Post-award conditions: N/A

Federal tax treatment: Undetermined, as the program has not yet been implemented.

Budgetary classification and funding: Discretionary. Amounts provided are subject to annual appropriations for FY2009 through FY2014. Funding has never been appropriated for the program.

Amounts discharged or repaid: N/A

Annual number of beneficiaries: N/A

□*R*□ *reports:* None.

Additional resources: None.

Pediatric Subspecialist Loan Repayment Program

Authority: *Statute:* PHSA, Title VII, §775; 42 U.S.C. §295f. *Regulations:* None. *CFDA:* None.

Federal administering agency: U.S. Department of Health and Human Services, Health Resources and Services Administration.

Purpose of program: To provide loan repayment to pediatric medical, surgical, and mental health subspecialists who provide care in a health professional shortage area (HPSA).

Eligible loan types: Any loans used to pay all or part of the cost of attendance at an institution of higher education, including loans incurred for undergraduate, graduate, or graduate medical education expenses. (This may include FFEL and Direct Loan program Subsidized Loans, Unsubsidized Loans, PLUS Loans, and Consolidation Loans; Perkins Loans; and private education loans).

Qualifying service or other activity: To qualify for loan repayment benefits, borrowers must be employed full-time as pediatric medical or surgical subspecialists or health professionals in child or adolescent mental and behavioral healthcare facilities. They must be employed in a HPSA or a medically underserved area. Borrowers may also be in training in one of these fields. Borrowers must complete at least two years of service, and they can agree to complete an additional year of service.

Maximum benefit amount: Up to $35,000 per year for a minimum of two years and a maximum of three years.

Restrictions on eligibility: U.S. citizens or legal permanent residents who are licensed to practice in one of the eligible fields or those who are enrolled in an accredited graduate program in one of these fields.

Post-award conditions: Undetermined, as the program has not yet been implemented.

Federal tax treatment: Undetermined, as the program has not yet been implemented.

Budgetary classification and funding: Discretionary. This program has not yet received any appropriations.

Annual amounts discharged or repaid: N/A

Annual number of beneficiaries: N/A

□*R*□ ***reports:*** CRS Report R41278, *Public Health, Workforce, Quality, and Related Provisions in ACA: Summary and Timeline*, coordinated by C. Stephen Redhead and Elayne J. Heisler; and CRS Report R43177, *Health Workforce Programs in Title VII of the Public Health Service Act*, by Bernice Reyes-Akinbileje.

Additional resources: Department of Health and Human Services, Health Resources and Services Administration, FY2014 Justification of Estimates for Appropriations Committees.

Nursing Workforce Development Student Loans: Loan Cancellation

Authority: *Statute:* PHSA §836(b)(3); 42 U.S.C. §297b(b)(3). *Regulations:* None. *CFDA:* None.

Federal administering agency: U.S. Department of Health and Human Services, Health Resources and Services Administration.

Purpose of program: To provide loan cancellation for borrowers who are employed as professional full-time nurses (including as a teacher, administrator, supervisor, or consultant in a nursing field) in public or nonprofit private agencies, institutions, or organizations.

Eligible loan types: Loans made to nursing students by schools from funds established under the statute (i.e., nursing education loans).

Qualifying service or other activity: To qualify for repayment benefits, borrowers must have received their loans before September 29, 1995 and must be employed as professional full-time nurses (including as a teacher, administrator, supervisor, or consultant in a nursing field) in a public or nonprofit private agencies, institutions, or organizations.

Maximum benefit amount: Up to 85% of the total loan made under the statute. 15% of the loan amount is repaid for each the first three years of service and 20% is paid for the fourth and fifth years of service.

Restrictions on eligibility: Undetermined, as the program has not yet been implemented.

Post-award conditions: Undetermined, as the program has not yet been implemented.

Federal tax treatment: Undetermined, as the program has not yet been implemented.

Budgetary classification and funding: Discretionary. The program has not yet received any appropriations.

Annual amounts discharged or repaid: N/A

Annual number of beneficiaries: N/A

☐*R*☐ ***report:*** CRS Report R41278, *Public Health, Workforce, Quality, and Related Provisions in ACA: Summary and Timeline*, coordinated by C. Stephen Redhead and Elayne J. Heisler.

Additional resources: None.

Nursing Workforce Development Student Loans: Loan Repayment

Authority: Statute: PHSA §836; 42 U.S.C. §297b(i). *Regulations:* None. *CFDA:* None.

Federal administering agency: U.S. Department of Health and Human Services, Health Resources and Services Administration.

Purpose of program: To provide loan repayment for nursing students who withdraw from nursing programs.

Eligible loan types: Loans made to nursing students by schools from funds established under the statute (i.e., nursing education loans).

Qualifying service or other activity: To qualify for repayment benefits, borrowers must have been unable to complete their studies, be in exceptionally needy circumstances, and have not resumed their studies within two years after they withdrew from their nursing studies.

Maximum benefit amount: Undetermined, as the program has not yet been implemented.

Restrictions on eligibility: Undetermined, as the program has not yet been implemented.

Post-award conditions: Undetermined, as the program has not yet been implemented.

Federal tax treatment: Undetermined, as the program has not yet been implemented.

Budgetary classification and funding: Discretionary. The program has not yet received any appropriations.

Annual amounts discharged or repaid: N/A

Annual number of beneficiaries: N/A

☐R☐ reports: None.

Additional resources: None.

Eligible Individual Student Loan Repayment

Authority: *Statute:* PHSA §847. 42 U.S.C. §297o. *Regulations:* None. *CFDA:* None.

Federal administering agency: U.S. Department of Health and Human Services, Health Resources and Services Administration.

Purpose of program: To increase the number of qualified nursing faculty.

Eligible loan types: Any loan used to pursue a nursing degree.

Qualifying service or other activity: To qualify for loan repayment, borrowers must be licensed nurses who have completed a master's or doctoral degree program (or are currently enrolled in such a program) and agree to serve as full-time nursing faculty members. Borrowers must complete at least four years of service during a six-year period that begins either when they receive their degrees or when they into loan repayment agreements.

Maximum benefit amount: Master's level nurses may receive up to $10,000 per year for a maximum total of $40,000. Doctoral degree nurses may receive $20,000 per year for a maximum total of $80,000. These amounts apply to FY2010 and FY2011 and are adjusted annually thereafter to account for cost-of-attendance increases.

Restrictions on eligibility: Undetermined, as the program has not yet been implemented, but at a minimum, borrowers must be U.S. citizens, nationals, or lawful permanent residents.

Post-award conditions: Borrowers must repay the total amount of all student loan repayments made on their behalf, plus interest calculated at the prevailing rate, if they do not complete their service agreement.

Federal tax treatment: Undetermined, as the program has not yet been implemented.

Budgetary classification and funding: Discretionary. Amounts provided are subject to annual appropriations for FY2010 through FY2014. The program has not yet received an appropriation.

Annual amounts discharged or repaid: N/A

Annual number of beneficiaries: N/A

☐R☐ reports: None.

Additional resources: None.

Loan Repayment for Public Service Employment in the Federal Government

Loan repayment programs to recruit and retain federal government employees are presented last in this appendix, as they are narrowly targeted to meet agency-specific recruitment and retention needs and, in general, are likely to be smaller in scale than the other loan repayment and forgiveness programs.

Student Loan Repayment Program for Senate Employees

Authority: Statute: Congressional Appropriations Act, 2002, Title I, §102; 2 U.S.C. §60c-5. *Regulations:* None. *CFDA:* None.

Federal administering agency: The Secretary of the Senate establishes standard procedures for program administration, and each employing office has the option of participating in the program.

Purpose of program: To recruit or retain qualified personnel.

Eligible loan types: FFEL and Direct Loan program Subsidized Loans, Unsubsidized Loans, PLUS Loans, and Consolidation Loans; Perkins Loans; and loans made available under PHSA Title VII-A and Title VIII-E.

Qualifying service or other activity: To qualify for repayment benefits, borrowers must be employees of the U.S. Senate or the Office of Congressional Accessibility Service. Borrowers must agree to complete at least one year of service and can enter into additional service agreements for successive one-year increments.

Maximum benefit amount: Up to $500 in any month and $40,000 in cumulative benefits.

Restrictions on eligibility: Repayment benefits are only available for the amount of a borrower's outstanding debt on the date that a service agreement is executed. Borrowers' salaries cannot exceed the ES-1 Senior Executive Service level of pay, and any loan payment made in any month cannot cause a borrower's monthly salary to be greater than $1/12^{th}$ of the statutorily maximum allowed salary. Loans to be repaid may not be in default or arrears. Loan repayment to employees of the Congressional Accessibility Service may not be provided for the same service used to qualify for benefits under the Government Employee Student Loan Repayment Program. A Member of the U.S. Senate is ineligible.

Post-award conditions: Borrowers must repay the amount of all student loan payments made on their behalf if they voluntarily separate, engage in misconduct, do not meet an acceptable level of performance, or violate a condition of a service agreement before they complete the required service period in a service agreement.

Federal tax treatment: The amount of student loan repayments received is included in gross income.

Budgetary classification and funding: Discretionary. Amounts provided are subject to annual appropriations for FY2002 and each fiscal year thereafter. Authorized amount for each employing office is 2% of the total amount appropriated for its administrative and clerical salaries.

Annual amount discharged or repaid: Information currently unavailable to CRS.

Annual number of beneficiaries: Information currently unavailable to CRS.

☐***R***☐***report:*** CRS Report RL31102, *Student Loan Repayment for Federal Employees*, by Barbara L. Schwemle and Lorraine H. Tong; archived.

Additional resources: None.

Student Loan Repayment Program for House Employees

Authority: Statute: Consolidated Appropriations Resolution, 2003, Div. H, Title I, §105; 2 U.S.C. §60c-6. *Regulations:* None. *CFDA:* None.

Federal administering agency: The Committee on House Administration establishes regulations for program administration, and each employing office has the option of participating in the program.

Purpose of program: To recruit or retain qualified personnel.

Eligible loan types: FFEL and Direct Loan program Subsidized Loans, Unsubsidized Loans, PLUS Loans, and Consolidation Loans; Perkins Loans; and loans made available under PHSA Title VII-A and Title VIII-E.

Qualifying service or other activity: To qualify for repayment benefits, borrowers must be employees of the U.S. House of Representatives. Borrowers must agree to complete at least one year of service.

Maximum benefit amount: Up to $833 in any month and $60,000 in cumulative benefits.

Restrictions on eligibility: Repayment benefits are only available for the amount of a borrower's outstanding debt on the date that a service agreement is executed. Loans to be repaid may not be in default or arrears. A Member of the U.S. House of Representatives (including a Delegate or Resident Commissioner to the Congress) is ineligible.

Post-award conditions: Borrowers must repay the amount of all student loan payments made on their behalf if they voluntarily separate or are involuntarily separated before they complete the required service period in the service agreement.

Federal tax treatment: The amount of student loan repayments received is included in gross income.

Budgetary classification and funding: Discretionary. Amounts provided are subject to annual appropriations for FY2003 and each fiscal year thereafter. Authorized amounts for each employing office is 3.5% of the amount available for office salaries and operating costs.

Annual amount discharged or repaid: Information currently unavailable to CRS.

Annual number of beneficiaries: Information currently unavailable to CRS.

☐*R*☐ *report:* CRS Report RL31102, *Student Loan Repayment for Federal Employees*, by Barbara L. Schwemle and Lorraine H. Tong; archived.

Additional resources: None.

Congressional Budget Office Student Loan Repayment

Authority: *Statute:* Congressional Appropriations Act, 2002, Title I, §127; 2 U.S.C. §610. *Regulations:* None. *CFDA:* None.

Federal administering agency: Congressional Budget Office.

Purpose of program: To recruit or retain qualified personnel.

Eligible loan type: Any student loan previously taken out by a qualifying employee (this may include FFEL and Direct Loan program Subsidized Loans, Unsubsidized Loans, PLUS Loans, and Consolidation Loans; and Perkins Loans).

Qualifying service or other activity: To qualify for repayment benefits, borrowers must be employees of the Congressional Budget Office.

Maximum benefit amount: Up to $6,000 per year and $40,000 in cumulative benefits.

Restrictions on eligibility: Repayment benefits are only available for the amount of a borrower's outstanding debts on the date a repayment agreement is executed.

Post-award conditions: N/A

Federal tax treatment: The amount of student loan repayments received is included in gross income.

Budgetary classification and funding: Discretionary. Information on previous amounts appropriated is currently unavailable to CRS.

Annual amount discharged or repaid: FY2009: $27,000. FY2010: $12,000. FY2011: $9,000. FY2012: $6,000. FY2013: $6,000.

Annual number of beneficiaries: FY2009: 5. FY2010: 2. FY2011: 2. FY2012: 1. FY2013: 1.

☐***R***☐ ***report:*** CRS Report RL31102, *Student Loan Repayment for Federal Employees*, by Barbara L. Schwemle and Lorraine H. Tong; archived.

Additional sources: None.

Government Employee Student Loan Repayment Program

Authority: Statute: National Defense Authorization Act for Fiscal Year 1991, Div. A, Title XII, §1206(b)(1); 5 U.S.C. §5379. *Regulations:* 5 C.F.R. §537. *CFDA:* None.

Federal administering agency: Individual executive agencies.

Purpose of program: To recruit or retain highly qualified personnel.

Eligible loan type: FFEL and Direct Loan program Subsidized Loans, Unsubsidized Loans, PLUS Loans, and Consolidation Loans; Perkins Loans; and loans made available under PHSA Title VII-A and PHSA Title VIII-E.

Qualifying service or other activity: To qualify for repayment benefits, borrowers must be employees of an Executive branch agency; certain Legislative branch agencies including the Government Accountability Office, the Government Printing Office, the Library of Congress, the Architect of the Capitol, the Botanic Garden, the Office of Congressional Accessibility; or government corporations (e.g., the Federal Deposit Insurance Corporation). Individual agencies can choose to provide repayment benefits to all employees or can target a particular occupation. Borrowers can be permanent employees; temporary employees who are serving appointments that can be converted to term or permanent appointments; term employees with at least three years left on their appointments; and employees serving in excepted appointments that can be converted to term, career, or career conditional appointments (e.g., Presidential Management Fellow, Career Intern). Borrowers must agree to complete at least three years of service.

Maximum benefit amount: Up to $10,000 per year and $60,000 in cumulative benefits.

Restrictions on eligibility: Repayment benefits are not available to borrowers who are employees in the excepted service because their position is confidential, policy-determining, policy-making, or policy-advocating in nature. Repayment benefits are only available for the amount of a borrower's outstanding debts on the date a repayment agreement is executed. An agency may not authorize student loan repayment benefits to recruit an individual from outside the agency who is currently in the federal service. An individual agency may specify that only student loans made within a certain timeframe are eligible for repayment.

Post-award conditions: Borrowers must repay employing agencies for the amount of all student loan payments made on their behalf if they voluntarily separate or are involuntarily terminated before the end of the service agreement. However, reimbursement may not be required if borrowers voluntarily enter into service with another agency.

Federal tax treatment: The amount of student loan repayments received is included in gross income.

Budgetary classification and funding: Discretionary. Amounts provided are subject to annual appropriations for each administering agency.

Annual amount discharged or repaid: Beginning in calendar year 2009, the Office of Personnel Management, which is the agency responsible for reporting on program, changed from fiscal year to calendar year reporting to synchronize and simplify agency reporting requirements. CY2009:

$61.8 million. CY2010: $85.7 million. CY2011: $71.8 million. CY2012: $70.3 million. CY2013: Information currently unavailable to CRS.

Annual number of beneficiaries: CY2009: 8,454 within 36 agencies. CY2010: 11,359 within 36 agencies. CY2011: 10,134 within 34 agencies. CY2012: 10,543 within 35 agencies. CY2013: Information currently unavailable to CRS.

☐*R*☐ *report:* CRS Report RL31102, *Student Loan Repayment for Federal Employees*, by Barbara L. Schwemle and Lorraine H. Tong; archived.

Additional resources: Office of Personnel Management, *Federal Student Loan Repayment Program Calendar Year 2012, Report to Congress,* http://www.opm.gov/policy-data-oversight/pay-leave/student-loan-repayment/reports/2012.pdf.

Defense Acquisition Workforce Student Loan Program

Authority: Statute: Defense Acquisition Workforce Improvement Act, Div. A, Title XII, §1202(a); 10 U.S.C. §1745. *Regulations*: None. *CFDA:* None.

Federal administering agency: Department of Defense.

Purpose of program: To recruit and retain qualified acquisition employees.

Eligible loan type: FFEL and Direct Loan program Subsidized Loans, Unsubsidized Loans, PLUS Loans, and Consolidation Loans; Perkins Loans; and loans made available under PHSA Title VII-A and Title VIII-E.

Qualifying service or other activity: To qualify for loan repayment benefits, borrowers must be military civilian acquisition personnel in the Department of Defense. Borrowers can be permanent employees, temporary employees who are serving appointments that can be converted to term or permanent appointments, term employees with at least three years left on their appointments, and employees serving in excepted appointments that can be converted to term, career, or career conditional appointments (e.g., Presidential Management Fellow, Career Intern). Borrowers must agree to complete at least three years of service.

Maximum benefit amount: Up to $10,000 per year and $60,000 in cumulative benefits.

Restrictions on eligibility: Benefits are only available for the amount of a borrower's outstanding student loan debt on the date a repayment agreement is executed.

Post-award conditions: Borrowers must reimburse employing agencies for the amount of all student loan payments made on their behalf if they voluntarily separate or are involuntarily terminated before they complete their service.

Federal tax treatment: The amount of student loan repayments received is included in gross income.

Budgetary classification and funding: Discretionary. Information on previous amounts appropriated is currently unavailable to CRS.

Annual amount discharged or repaid: Information currently unavailable to CRS.

Annual number of beneficiaries: Information currently unavailable to CRS.

☐R☐ reports: None.

Additional resources: None.

Armed Forces Educational Loan Repayment Program: Enlisted Members on Active Duty in Specified Military Specialties

Authority: Statute: Department of Defense Authorization Act, 1986, Title VI, Part F, §671(a)(1); 10 U.S.C. §2171. *Regulations:* None. *CFDA:* None.

Federal administering agency: Department of Defense, applicable military branch.

Purpose of program: To recruit individuals to serve in certain military occupational specialties.

Eligible loan type: FFEL and Direct Loan program Subsidized Stafford Loans, Unsubsidized Stafford Loans, PLUS Loans, and Consolidation Loans; Perkins loans; and state and private education loans.

Qualifying service or other activity: To qualify for repayment benefits, borrowers must perform active duty in an officer program or military specialty specified by the Secretary of Defense. Borrowers must complete at least one year of service, and loan repayments are made for each complete year of service. Both officers and enlisted members on active duty are eligible.

Maximum benefit amount: The greater of 33 1/3% of a borrower's outstanding student loan debt or $1,500 for each year of service. The Army, Army Judge Advocate General Corps, and Navy offer up to $65,000 in cumulative benefits; the Air Force offers up to $10,000 in cumulative benefits, and the Marine Corps offers up to $30,000 in cumulative benefits.

Restrictions on eligibility: Benefits are only available for the amount of a borrower's outstanding student loan debt on the date a repayment agreement is executed; outstanding accrued interest and capitalized interest is not repaid.

Post-award conditions: Borrowers must repay an amount equal to the unearned portion of loan repayments if they fail to complete their service.

Federal tax treatment: The amount of student loan repayments received is included in gross income.

Budgetary classification and funding: Discretionary. Amounts appropriated are included as part of the relevant military service component's personnel appropriation.

Annual Amount ☐ischarged or repaid:

Army. FY2009: $68 million. FY2010: $56.9 million. FY2011: $98.7 million. FY2012: $124.8 million. FY2013: $114.4 million.

Navy. FY2009: $9.7 million. FY2010: $8.4 million. FY2011: $8.4 million. FY2012: $11.6 million. FY2013: $14.2 million.

Marine Corps. FY2009: $1.5 million. FY2010: $5.9 million. FY2011: $12 million. FY2012: $11.4 million. FY2013: $7.3 million.

Marine Corps, Judge Advocate Officers. FY2009: $530,000. FY2010: $590,000. FY2011: $734,000. FY2012: 720,000. FY2013: $800,000.

Air Force. FY2009: $4.4 million. FY2010: $7.5 million. FY2011: $7.9 million. FY2012: $9.5 million. FY2013: $4.8 million.

Air Force, Judge Advocate General Corps. FY2009: $0. FY2010: $217,000. FY2011: $2.5 million. FY2012: $3.9 million. FY2013: $5.2 million.

Annual number of beneficiaries:

Army. FY2009: 12,447. FY2010: 10,559. FY2011: 15,614. FY2012: 8,500. FY2103: 9,954.

Navy. FY2009: 1,317. FY2010: 909. FY2011: 732. FY2012: 486. FY2013: 566.

Marine Corps. FY2009: 265. FY2010: 500. FY2011: 1,200. FY2012: 486. FY2013: 729.

Marine Corps Judge Advocate Officers: FY2009: 53. FY2010: 59. FY2011: 73. FY2012: 62. FY2013: 80.

Air Force. FY2009: 1,250. FY2010: 1,762. FY2011: 1,315. FY2012: 1,382. FY2013: 1,194.

Air Force, Judge Advocate General Corps. FY2009: 0. FY2010: 10. FY2011: 115. FY2012: 182. FY2013: 242.

☐R☐reports: None.

Additional resources: National Council of Higher Education Loan Programs, Program Regulations Committee, "Matrix of Department of Defense (DOD) and Other Federal Student Loan Repayment Programs," February 2, 2012, http://c.ymcdn.com/sites/www.ncher.us/resource/ collection/F4EAF7F5-F223-4EC9-9C0E-5511898606A6/02-08- 13_DOD_Repayment_Matrix.pdf.

Education Loan Repayment Program: Members of the Selected Reserve

Authority: Statute: National Defense Authorization Act for Fiscal Year 1996, Div. A, Title XV, Subtitle G, §1079(b); 10 U.S.C. §16301. *Regulations:* None. *CFDA:* None.

Federal administering agency: Department of Defense, applicable military branch.

Purpose of program: To serve as bonus pay for service in the Selected Reserve.

Eligible loan type: FFEL and Direct Loan program Subsidized Loans, Unsubsidized Loans, PLUS Loans, and Consolidation; Perkins loans; and state and private education loans.

Qualifying service or other activity: To qualify for repayment benefits, borrowers must serve as members of the Selected Reserve of the Ready Reserve of an armed force in a reserve component, in an officer program, or in a military specialty authorized by the Secretary of Defense. Loan repayments are made for each complete year of service.

Maximum benefit allowed: The greater of 15% of a borrower's outstanding student loans or $500 for each year of service, plus any interest that accrues during the current year. The Army offers up to either $10,000 or $20,000 in cumulative benefits, depending on the borrower's military occupational specialty; the Army National Guard offers up to $50,000 in cumulative benefits, and the Air National Guard offers up to $20,000 in cumulative benefits.

Restrictions on eligibility: A loan must have been made before the borrower served in an armed force.

Post-award conditions: Borrowers must repay an amount equal to the unearned portion of student loan repayment if they fail to complete their service.

Federal tax treatment: The amount of student loan repayments received is included in gross income.

Budgetary classification and funding: Discretionary. Amounts appropriated are included as part of the relevant military service component's personnel appropriation.

Annual amount discharged or repaid:

Army Reserve. FY2009: $10.7 million. FY2010: $8.4 million. FY2011: $5.3 million. FY2012: $5.8 million. FY2013: 16.7 million.

Army National Guard. FY2009: $34.6 million. FY2010: $6.1 million. FY2011: $20.7 million. FY2012: $27.8 million. FY2013 (estimated): $28.8 million.

Air National Guard. FY2009: Information currently unavailable to CRS. FY2010: $12.3 million. FY2011: $12.8 million. FY2012: $10.7 million. FY2013 (estimated): $10.8 million.

Annual number of beneficiaries:

Army Reserve. FY2009: 8,295. FY2010: 6,538. FY2011: 2,275. FY2012: 2,486. FY2013: 7,116.

Army National Guard. FY2009: 30,573. FY2010: 5,437. FY2011: 11,231. FY2012: 15,073. FY2013 (estimated): 15,603.

Air National Guard. FY2009: Information currently unavailable to CRS. FY2010: 3,528. FY2011: 3,665. FY2012: 3,061. FY2013 (estimated): 3,099.

□*R*□ *reports:* None.

Additional resources: National Council of Higher Education Loan Programs, Program Regulations Committee, "Matrix of Department of Defense (DOD) and Other Federal Student Loan Repayment Programs," February 2, 2012, http://c.ymcdn.com/sites/www.ncher.us/resource/collection/F4EAF7F5-F223-4EC9-9C0E-5511898606A6/02-08-13_DOD_Repayment_Matrix.pdf.

Education Loan Repayment Program: Health Professions Officers Serving in Selected Reserve with Wartime Critical Medical Skill Shortages

Authority: Statute: Department of Defense Authorization Act, 1986; 10 U.S.C. §16302. *Regulations:* None. *CFDA:* None.

Federal administering agency: Department of Defense, applicable military branch. The program has been implemented by the Army Reserve, the Army National Guard, and the Air National Guard.

Purpose of program: To provide loan repayment to health professionals who provide healthcare in specialties that meet identified wartime skill shortages.

Eligible loan types: FFEL and Direct Loan program Subsidized Loans, Unsubsidized Loans, Graduate PLUS Loans, Consolidation Loans; Perkins Loans; and loans made available under PHSA Title VII-A and PHSA Title VIII-B; loans made through the Primary Care Loan Program; and commercial loans used to pursue a health profession education. Parent PLUS loans are ineligible.

Qualifying service or other activity: To qualify for repayment benefits, borrowers must perform satisfactory service in the Selected Reserve of an armed force and be qualified or enrolled in an educational program leading to such qualifications in a health profession that the Secretary of Defense determines to be critically needed in order to meet identified wartime combat medical skills shortages. Borrowers must complete one year of service for each year of loan repayment received.

Maximum benefit amount: Up to $60,000 per year. Annual amounts vary by military branch and health professions receiving the loan repayment benefits.

Restrictions on eligibility: Borrowers must be commissioned officers on or before December 31, 2011. Loans to be repaid may not be in default and must be more than one year old.

Post-award conditions: N/A

Federal tax treatment: The amount of student loan repayments received is included in gross income.

Budgetary classification and funding: Discretionary. Amounts appropriated are included as part of the relevant military service component's personnel appropriation.

Annual amounts discharged or repaid:

Army Reserve. FY2009: 3.0 million. FY2010: $19.6 million. FY2011: $4.7 million. FY2012: $8.8 million. FY2013: $15.6 million.

Army National Guard. FY2009: 901,000. FY2010: $19.2 million. FY2011: $709,000. FY2012: $3.9 million. FY2013: $568,000.

Navy Reserve. FY2009: $800,000. FY2010: $1.2 million. FY2011: $1.7 million. FY2012: $824,000. FY2013: $1.0 million.

Air Force Reserve. FY2009: $1.0 million.. FY2010: $760,000. FY2011: $1.8 million. FY2012: $2.9 million. FY2013: $3.5 million.

Air National Guard. FY2009: 1.2 million. FY2010: $2.2 million. FY2011: $2.5 million. FY2012: $3.8 million. FY2013: $1.5 million.

Annual number of beneficiaries:

Army Reserve. FY2009: 199. FY2010: 1,120. FY2011: 260. FY2012: 470. FY2013: 808.

Army National Guard. FY2009: 53. FY2010: 966. FY2011: 35. FY2012: 146. FY2013: 28.

Navy Reserve. FY2009: 77. FY2010: 75. FY2011: 98. FY2012: 47. FY2013: 65.

Air Force Reserve. FY2009: 64. FY2010: 51. FY2011: 65. FY2012: 85. FY2013: 88.

Air National Guard. FY2009: 65 FY2010: 126. FY2011: 136. FY2012: 217. FY2013: 78.

☐R☐ reports: None.

Additional resources: Department of Defense, Fiscal Year 2014 Budget Estimates: Operation and Maintenance Procurement, Research, Development, Test, and Evaluation, Volume I: Justification of Estimates, Washington, DC, April 2013, http://comptroller.defense.gov/defbudget/fy2014/ budget_justification/pdfs/09_Defense_Health_Program/ FY2014_DHP_Budget_Estimates_Vol_1.pdf.

Education Loan Repayment Program: Chaplains Serving in the Selected Reserve

Authority: Statute: National Defense Authorization Act for Fiscal Year 2006, Div. A, Title VI, Subtitle F, §§684(a), 687(c)(14); 10 U.S.C. §16303. *Regulations:* None. *CFDA:* None.

Federal administering agency: Department of Defense, applicable military branch.

Purpose of program: To maintain adequate numbers of chaplains in the Selected Reserve.

Eligible loan type: Any loan used to pay all or part of the cost of attendance at an institution of higher education (this may include FFEL and Direct Loan program Subsidized Loans, Unsubsidized Loans, PLUS Loans, and Consolidation Loans; Perkins Loans; and private education loans).

Qualifying service or other activity: To qualify for repayment benefits, borrowers must satisfy the requirements for accessioning and commissioning of chaplains and be fully qualified for or appointed as chaplains in a reserve component. Borrowers must also enter into a written agreement with the relevant military branch and serve at least three years in the Selected Reserve.

Maximum benefit allowed: Up to $10,000 in the first year and $20,000 in total for each three year period of obligated service.

Restrictions on eligibility: Borrowers accessioned into the Chaplain Candidate Program cannot receive repayment benefits.

Post-award conditions: Borrowers must repay an amount equal to the unearned portion of loan repayments if they fail to complete their service.

Federal tax treatment: The amount of student loan repayments received is included in gross income.

Budgetary classification and funding: Discretionary. Amounts appropriated are included as part of the relevant military service component's personnel appropriation.

Annual amount discharged or repaid: Air National Guard, FY2009: 550,000. FY2010: $696,000. FY2011: $235,000. FY2012: $712,000. FY2013: $408,000.

Annual number of beneficiaries: Air National Guard, FY2009: 60. FY2010: 82. FY2011: 32. FY2012: 121. FY2013: 62.

□R□reports: None.

Additional resources: None.

Federal Food, Drug, and Cosmetic Act Loan Repayment Program

Authority: *Statute:* Federal Food, Drug, and Cosmetic Act §1005; 21 U.S.C. §395. *Regulations*: None. *CFDA:* None.

Federal administering agency: U.S. Department of Health and Human Services, Food and Drug Administration (FDA).

Purpose of program: To recruit appropriately qualified health professionals to conduct research as employees of the FDA.

Eligible loan types: Government and private loans obtained for tuition, other educational expenses, and reasonable living expenses for undergraduate education, graduate education, or both.

Qualifying service or other activity: To qualify for repayment benefits, borrowers must be appropriately qualified health professionals who conduct research while FDA employees. Borrowers must complete at least three years of service.

Maximum benefit amount: Up to $20,000 per year.

Restrictions on eligibility: Borrowers must have a substantial amount of education loans relative to income (i.e., debt is more than 20% of borrower's annual federal salary).

Post-award conditions: Borrowers must pay an amount equal to the sum of: (1) the amount of loan repayments paid to the participant for a period of service not completed; (2) $7,500 multiplied by the number of months of service not completed; and (3) the interest on the sum of (1) and (2) calculated at the maximum prevailing rate—as determined by the Treasury—from the date of the contract breach if they do not complete their service commitment.

Federal tax treatment: The amount of student loan repayments received is excluded from gross income if the loan meets certain conditions.

Budgetary classification and funding: Discretionary.

Annual amounts discharged or repaid: FY2009: $849,000. FY2010: $1.7 million. FY2011: $1.6 million. FY2012: $1.7 million. FY2013: $2.2 million.

Annual number of beneficiaries: FY2009: 101. FY2010: 188. FY2011: 190. FY2012: 194. FY2013: 248.

☐R☐ reports: None.

Additional resources: None.

Education Debt Reduction Program

Authority: *Statute:* Caregivers and Veterans Omnibus Health Services Act of 2010, Title III, §301, P.L. 111-136; 38 U.S.C. §§7681-7683. *Regulations:* None. *CFDA:* None.

Federal administering agency: U.S. Department of Veterans Affairs (VA), Veterans Health Administration (VHA).

Purpose of program: To recruit and retain qualified health professionals to serve in positions within the VHA for which recruitment or retention is difficult.

Eligible loan types: Loans used to pay all or part of the cost of tuition and reasonable educational and living expenses to obtain a health professional degree (this may include FFEL and Direct Loan program Subsidized Loans, Unsubsidized Loans, PLUS Loans, and Consolidation Loans; Perkins Loans; and private education loans).

Qualifying service or other activity: To qualify for repayment benefits, borrowers must be VHA employees who provide direct patient care or services incident to direct patient care services for which the recruitment and retention of qualified health professions is difficult. Eligible borrowers include those in the following fields: audiology, dentistry, dental hygiene, nursing, occupational therapy, optometry, medicine (including physician assistants), podiatry, physical therapy (including assistants), social work, speech pathology, radiological technology, and respiratory therapy. Borrowers must have been appointed to the VA within the six months prior and have acceptable performance ratings in their positions.

Maximum benefit amount: Up to $60,000 over a total of five years of service, but repayment amounts may not exceed $12,000 in the fourth or fifth year of service. Borrowers may not receive annual loan repayment amounts that would exceed the amount of the principal and interest on their education or training loans.

Restrictions on eligibility: Repayment benefits are awarded on a competitive basis, with priority given to the health professions that are most difficult positions to fill.

Post-award conditions: N/A

Federal tax treatment: The amount of student loan repayments received is included in gross income.

Budgetary classification and funding: Discretionary. Funding for this program is derived from amounts available to the Secretary of the VHA for medical services.

Annual amounts discharged or repaid: FY2009: $13.7 million. FY2010: $17 million. FY2011: $17.3 million. FY2012: $19.2 million. FY2013: $16.6 million.

Annual number of beneficiaries: FY2009-FY2012: Information currently unavailable to CRS. FY2013: 2,678.

☐*R*☐*reports:* None.

Additional resources: U.S. Department of Veterans Affairs, Congressional Submission, FY2015 Funding and FY2016 Advance Appropriations Request, Volume II, Medical Programs and Information Technology Programs, Washington, DC, http://www.va.gov/budget/docs/summary/ Fy2015-VolumeII-MedicalProgramsAndInformationTechnology.pdf; and Department of Veterans Affairs, Veterans Health Administration, Workforce Succession Strategic Plan 2011-2016.

National Institutes of Health Intramural Loan Repayment Program: Acquired Immune Deficiency Syndrome (AIDS) Research

Authority: Statute: PHSA, Title IV, §487A; 42 U.S.C. §288-1; *Regulations:* None. *CFDA:* 93.936.

Federal administering agency: U.S. Department of Health and Human Services, National Institutes of Health (NIH).

Purpose of program: To help assure an adequate supply of qualified health professionals in Acquired Immunodeficiency Syndrome (AIDS) research.

Eligible loan types: FFEL and Direct Loan program Subsidized Loans, Unsubsidized Loans, PLUS Loans (made after July 1, 2006), and Consolidation Loans; loans made available under PHSA Title VII-A and Title VIII-E; loans made or guaranteed by a state, the District of Columbia, the Commonwealth of Puerto Rico, or a territory or possession of the United States; loans made by academic institutions; and private education loans including MEDLOANS. PLUS loans made to parents are ineligible.

Qualifying service or other activity: To qualify for repayment benefits, borrowers must be employees of the NIH—appointed under the Federal Civil Service (Title V or Title 42) or under the Commissioned Corps of the U.S. Public Health Service—and must conduct clinical research on AIDS. Borrowers must complete at least two years of service and can agree to complete an additional year of service.

Maximum benefit amount: Up to $35,000 per year.

Restrictions on eligibility: Repayment benefits are awarded on a competitive basis, based on NIH's research priorities. Borrowers must be U.S. citizens or permanent legal residents and must have obtained a health professional doctoral degree (i.e., a PhD; a doctorate in medicine, osteopathic medicine, dentistry, pharmacy, veterinary medicine; or an equivalent) or a bachelor's of science in nursing, a physician assistant degree, or an associate degree in nursing. Borrowers must have qualifying educational debt in excess of 20% of their annual NIH base salary, and borrowers with a federal judgment or lien against their property are ineligible. Borrowers must not have received support from any of the following programs: Physicians Shortage Area Scholarship Program, National Research Service Award Program, Public Health Service Scholarship Program, National Health Service Corps Scholarship Program, Primary Care Loan Program, Armed Forces (Army, Navy, or Air Force) Professions Scholarship Program, and the Indian Health Service Scholarship Program; borrowers who have received a deferral from one of these programs may be eligible.

Post-award conditions: Borrowers must pay $7,500 per month of service not completed plus all the amounts paid on their behalf for months that were not served. Borrowers must also pay interest on the amount owed, with interest accruing from the date of breach. The U.S. government is entitled to recover not less than $31,000. Borrowers may terminate renewal contracts at any time without penalties. Loan repayments are prorated and terminated on the date that research stops.

Federal tax treatment: Borrowers can receive an additional 39% of the total loan repayment amount for federal income tax liability.

Budgetary classification and funding: Discretionary. Previous amounts appropriated (for all NIH intramural loan repayment and scholarship programs), FY2009: $7.4 million. FY2010: $7.5 million. FY2011: $7.4 million. FY2012: $7.4 million.

Annual amounts discharged or repaid: FY2009: $48,000. FY2010: $285,000. FY2011: $234,000. FY2012: $193,000.

Annual number of beneficiaries: FY2009: 0 new awards and 4 renewals. FY2010: 1 new award and 6 renewals. FY2011: 1 new award and 6 renewals. FY2012: 2 new and 3 renewals.

☐R☐reports: CRS Report R41705, *The National Institutes of Health (NIH): Background and Congressional Issues*, by Judith A. Johnson.

Additional resources: Various years of Department of Health and Human Services, National Institutes of Health, Justification of Estimates for Congressional Committees, Office of the Director, Washington, DC and various years of the NIH Intramural Loan Repayment Annual Report, http://www.lrp.nih.gov/reports_and_statistics/index.aspx.

National Institutes of Health Intramural Loan Repayment Program: General Research

Authority: Statute: PHSA, Title IV, §487C; 42 U.S.C. §§288-3. *Regulations*: None. *CFDA:* 93.232.

Federal administering agency: U.S. Department of Health and Human Services, National Institutes of Health (NIH).

Purpose of program: To recruit qualified health professionals to conduct research as NIH employees.

Eligible loan types: FFEL and Direct Loan program Subsidized Loans, Unsubsidized Loans, PLUS Loans (made after July 1, 2006), and Consolidation Loans; loans made available under PHSA Title VII-A and Title VIII-E; loans made or guaranteed by a state, the District of Columbia, the Commonwealth of Puerto Rico, or a territory or possession of the United States; loans made by academic institutions; and private education loans including MEDLOANS.

Qualifying service or other activity: To qualify for repayment benefits, borrowers must be employees of the NIH—appointed under the Federal Civil Service (Title V or Title 42) or under the Commissioned Corps of the U.S. Public Health Service—and must conduct general research. Borrowers must complete at least three years of service and can agree to complete an additional year of service.

Maximum benefit amount: Up to $35,000 per year.

Restrictions on eligibility: Repayment benefits are awarded on a competitive basis, based on NIH's research priorities. Borrowers must be U.S. citizens or permanent legal residents and must have obtained a health professional doctoral degree (i.e., a PhD; a doctorate in medicine, osteopathic medicine, dentistry, pharmacy, veterinary medicine; or an equivalent) or a must have obtained a bachelor's of science in nursing, a physician assistant degree, or an associate degree in nursing. Borrowers must have qualifying educational debt in excess of 20% of their annual NIH base salary, and borrowers with a federal judgment or lien against their property are ineligible. Borrowers must not have received support from any of the following programs: Physicians Shortage Area Scholarship Program, National Research Service Award Program, Public Health Service Scholarship Program, National Health Service Corps Scholarship Program, Primary Care Loan Program, Armed Forces (Army, Navy, or Air Force) Professions Scholarship Program, and the Indian Health Service Scholarship Program; borrowers who have received a deferral from one of these programs may be eligible.

Post-award conditions: Borrowers must pay $7,500 per month of service not completed, plus all the amounts paid on their behalf for months that were not served. Borrowers must also pay interest on the amount owed, with interest accruing from the date of breach. The U.S. government is entitled to recover not less than $31,000. Borrowers may terminate renewal contracts at any time without penalties. Loan repayments are prorated and terminated on the date that research stops.

Federal tax treatment: Borrowers can receive an additional 39% of the total loan repayment amount for federal income tax liability.

Budgetary classification and funding: Discretionary. Previous amounts appropriated (for all NIH intramural loan repayment and scholarship programs), FY2009: $7.4 million. FY2010: $7.5 million. FY2011: $7.4 million. FY2012: $7.4 million.

Annual amounts discharged or repaid: FY2009: $3.5 million. FY2010: $3.2 million. FY2011: $2.9 million. FY2012: $3.0 million.

Annual number of beneficiaries: FY2009: 22 new awards and 34 renewals. FY2010: 16 new and 38 renewals. FY2011: 14 new awards and 41 renewals. FY2012: 18 new awards and 42 renewals.

☐*R*☐*report:* CRS Report R41705, *The National Institutes of Health (NIH): Background and Congressional Issues*, by Judith A. Johnson.

Additional resources: Various years of Department of Health and Human Services, National Institutes of Health, Justification of Estimates for Congressional Committees, Office of the Director, Washington, DC and various years of the NIH Intramural Loan Repayment Annual Report, http://www.lrp.nih.gov/reports_and_statistics/index.aspx.

National Institutes of Health Intramural Loan Repayment Program: General Research Loan Repayment Program for Accreditation Council For Graduate Medical Education (ACGME) Fellows

tatute: PHSA, Title IV, §487C; 42 U.S.C. §§288-3. *Regulations:* None. *CFDA:* 93.232.

Federal administering agency: U.S. Department of Health and Human Services, National Institutes of Health (NIH).

Purpose of program: To help the NIH recruit fellowship trainees to conduct their training at the NIH.

Eligible loan types: FFEL and Direct Loan program Subsidized Loans, Unsubsidized Loans, PLUS Loans (made after July 1, 2006), and Consolidation Loans; loans made available under PHSA Title VII-A and Title VIII-E; loans made or guaranteed by a state, the District of Columbia, the Commonwealth of Puerto Rico, or a territory or possession of the United States; loans made by academic institutions; and private education loans including MEDLOANS. PLUS loans made to parents are ineligible.

Qualifying service or other activity: To qualify for repayment benefits, borrowers must be completing their medical fellowship training at the NIH. Borrowers must complete at three years of service.

Maximum benefit amount: Up to $17,000 per year.

Restrictions on eligibility: Repayment benefits are awarded on a competitive basis, based on the NIH's research priorities. Borrowers must be U.S. citizens or permanent legal residents and must have obtained a doctorate in medicine or osteopathic medicine. Borrowers must have qualifying educational debt in excess of 20% of their annual NIH base salary, and borrowers with a federal judgment or lien against their property are ineligible. Borrowers must not have received support from any of the following programs: Physicians Shortage Area Scholarship Program, National Research Service Award Program, Public Health Service Scholarship Program, National Health Service Corps Scholarship Program, Primary Care Loan Program, Armed Forces (Army, Navy, or Air Force) Professions Scholarship Program, and the Indian Health Service Scholarship Program; borrowers who have received a deferral from one of these programs may be eligible.

Post-award conditions: Borrowers must pay $7,500 per month of service not completed plus all the amounts paid on their behalf for months that were not served. Borrowers must also pay interest on the amount owed, with interest accruing from the date of breach. The federal government is entitled to recover not less than $31,000. Borrowers may terminate renewal contracts at any time without penalties. Loan repayments are prorated and terminated on the date that research stops.

Federal tax treatment: Borrowers can receive an additional 39% of the total loan repayment amount for federal income tax liability.

Budgetary classification and funding: Discretionary. Previous amounts appropriated (for all NIH intramural loan repayment and scholarship programs), FY2009: $7.4 million. FY2010: $7.5 million. FY2011: $7.4 million. FY2012: $7.4 million.

Annual amounts discharged or repaid: FY2009: $1.49 million. FY2010: $1.57 million. FY2011: $1.66 million. FY2012: $1.13 million.

Annual number of beneficiaries: FY2009: 17 new awards. FY2010: 18 new awards. FY2011: 20 new awards. FY2012: 17 new.

□*R*□ *report:* CRS Report R41705, *The National Institutes of Health (NIH): Background and Congressional Issues*, by Judith A. Johnson.

Additional resources: Various years of Department of Health and Human Services, National Institutes of Health, Justification of Estimates for Congressional Committees, Office of the Director, Washington, DC and various years of the NIH Intramural Loan Repayment Annual Report, http://www.lrp.nih.gov/reports_and_statistics/index.aspx.

National Institutes of Health Intramural Loan Repayment Program: Clinical Researchers from Disadvantaged Backgrounds

Authority: Statute: PHSA, Title IV, §487E; 42 U.S.C. §288-5. *Regulations:* 42 C.F.R. §68a. *CFDA:* 93.220.

Federal administering agency: U.S. Department of Health and Human Services, National Institutes of Health (NIH).

Purpose of program: To recruit highly qualified health professionals from disadvantaged backgrounds to serve as clinical researchers.

Eligible loan types: FFEL and Direct Loan program Subsidized Loans, Unsubsidized Loans, PLUS Loans (made after July 1, 2006), and Consolidation Loans; loans made available under PHSA Title VII-A and Title VIII-E; loans made or guaranteed by a state, the District of Columbia, the Commonwealth of Puerto Rico, or a territory or possession of the United States; loans made by academic institutions; and private education loans including MEDLOANS.

Qualifying service or other activity: To qualify for repayment benefits, borrowers must be employees of the NIH—appointed under the Federal Civil Service (Title V or Title 42) or under the Commissioned Corps of the U.S. Public Health Service—and must conduct clinical research. Borrowers must be from disadvantaged backgrounds based on environmental or family economic circumstances. Borrowers must complete at least two years of service and can agree to complete an additional year of service.

Maximum benefit amount: Up to $35,000 per year.

Restrictions on eligibility: Repayment benefits are awarded on a competitive basis, based on NIH's research priorities. Borrowers must be U.S. citizens or permanent legal residents and must have obtained a health professional doctoral degree (i.e., a PhD; a doctorate in medicine, osteopathic medicine, dentistry, pharmacy, veterinary medicine; or an equivalent) or a must have obtained a bachelor's of science in nursing, a physician assistant degree, or an associate degree in nursing. Borrowers must have qualifying educational debt in excess of 20% of their annual NIH base salary, and borrowers with a federal judgment or lien against their property are ineligible. Borrowers must not have received support from any of the following programs: Physicians Shortage Area Scholarship Program, National Research Service Award Program, Public Health Service Scholarship Program, National Health Service Corps Scholarship Program, Primary Care Loan Program, Armed Forces (Army, Navy, or Air Force) Professions Scholarship Program, and the Indian Health Service Scholarship Program; borrowers who have received a deferral from one of these programs may be eligible.

Post-award conditions: Borrowers must pay $7,500 per month of service not completed, plus all the amounts paid on their behalf for months that were not served. Borrowers must also pay interest on the amount owed, with interest accruing from the date of breach. The U.S. government is entitled to recover not less than $31,000. Borrowers may terminate renewal contracts at any time without penalties. Loan repayments are prorated and terminated on the date that research stops.

Federal tax treatment: Borrowers can receive an additional 39% of the total loan repayment amount for federal income tax liability.

Budgetary classification and funding: Discretionary. Previous amounts appropriated (for all intramural loan repayment and scholarship programs), FY2009: $7.4 million. FY2010: $7.5 million. FY2011: $7.4 million. FY2012: $7.4 million.

Annual amounts discharged or repaid: FY2009: $77,500. FY2010: $251,400; FY2011: $64,300; FY2012: $6,400.

Annual number of beneficiaries: FY2009: 0 new awards and 3 renewals. FY2010: 1 new award and 4 renewals. FY2011: 0 new awards and 4 renewals. FY2012: 0 new and 2 renewals.

☐*R*☐ ***report:*** CRS Report R41705, *The National Institutes of Health (NIH): Background and Congressional Issues*, by Judith A. Johnson.

Additional resources: Various years of Department of Health and Human Services, National Institutes of Health, Justification of Estimates for Congressional Committees, Office of the Director, Washington, DC and various years of the NIH Intramural Loan Repayment Annual Report, http://www.lrp.nih.gov/reports_and_statistics/index.aspx.

National and Community Service Grant Program, Use of Educational Award to Repay Outstanding Student Loans

Authority: *Statute:* National and Community Service Trust Act of 1993, Title I, Subtitle A, §102(a); 42 U.S.C. §12604. *Regulations:* 45 C.F.R. §2526 et seq. *CFDA:* None.

Federal administering agency: Corporation for National and Community Service (the Corporation), the National Service Trust.

Purpose of program: To encourage citizens to participate in national service programs intended to meet unmet human, educational, environmental, and public safety needs.

Eligible loan type: FFEL and Direct Loan Subsidized Loans Unsubsidized Loans, PLUS Loans, and Consolidation Loans; Perkins loans; loans made available under PHSA Title VII-A and Title VIII-E; and any other loan determined by an institution of higher education to be necessary to cover a student's educational expenses and made, insured, guaranteed by an eligible lender.

Qualifying service or other activity: To qualify for repayment benefits, borrowers must successfully complete service in either the AmeriCorps State or National, the National Civilian Community Corps (NCCC), or Volunteers in Service to America (VISTA) programs and be eligible to receive a national service educational award, summer of service educational award, or silver scholar educational award from the National Service Trust. Additionally, within the NCCC, participants may serve in FEMA Corps, which is a partnership between FEMA and the Corporation under which participants serve solely devoted to disaster preparedness, response, and recovery.

Maximum benefit allowed: An amount equal to the maximum Pell Grant award in effect at the beginning of the fiscal year in which the Corporation approves an individual's service position (in either AmeriCorps, NCCC, VISTA, or FEMA Corps). For national service and silver scholar educational awards, borrowers cannot receive an amount greater than two full-time education awards. Prorated awards are also available based on term of service. For instance, in FY2013, the award amounts for term of service were the following:

- Full-time service (at least 1,700 hours of service): $5,550

- One-year half time service (at least 900 hours of service): $2,775

- Reduced half time (at least 675 hours of service): $2,114

- Quarter time (at least 450 hours of service): $1,468

- Minimum time (at least 300 hours of service): $1,175

Restrictions on eligibility: Award recipients must use awards within seven years of the date the term of service was completed. Summer of service participants must use awards within 10 years of the date the term was completed.

Post-award conditions: N/A

Federal tax treatment: The amount of education awards received is included in gross income.

Budgetary classification and funding: Discretionary. Amounts provided are subject to annual appropriations for FY2010 through FY2014. Previous amounts appropriated, FY2009: $131 million. ARRA: $40 million. FY2010: $197 million. FY2011: $199 million. FY2012: $211.8 million. FY2013: $200.7 million. In addition to the Corporation's annual appropriations, as part of the FEMA Corps partnership, FEMA makes a contribution to the Trust towards participants' education awards (National Service Cost Share; NSCS).

Annual amount discharged or repaid: Beneficiaries of the program can use their awards up to seven years after they are awarded, therefore, the dollar amount reported reflects the amount of money *used* by beneficiaries in a particular program year (PY). A program year refers to service positions awarded to participants with a particular fiscal year's funds. Positions are often filled in time periods after the year in which they are awarded (e.g., money is granted to an AmeriCorps State program in FY2011, but not all positions available in the program are filled until FY2012). The PY2013 figure represents the amount of awards used as of June 2013.

Education awards can be used to pay current tuition expenses and to repay student loans, therefore, the numbers reported include money expended to both pay current tuition expenses and to repay student loans.

Program Year (PY)2009: $120.8 million. ARRA: $25.5 million. PY2010: $143.7 million. PY2011: $100.7 million. 2012 NSCS: $58,336. PY2012: $8.4 million. PY2013 (as of June 2013): $3,241.

Annual number of beneficiaries: Because program beneficiaries have up to seven years to use an education award after it is made, the annual beneficiaries presented here reflect the number of AmeriCorps State and National, NCC, VISTA, and FEMA Corps participants who earned education awards. The PY2013 figure represents the number of participants who earned education awards as of June 2013.

PY2009: 58,205. ARRA: 2,395. PY2010: 73,727. PY2011: 65,416. 2012 NSCS: 361 PY2012: 17,136. PY2013 (as of June 2013): 28.

☐*R*☐ ***report:*** CRS Report RL33931, *The Corporation for National and Community Service: Overview of Programs and Funding,* by Abigail B. Rudman and Benjamin Collins.

Additional resources: None.

Capitol Police Student Loan Repayment

Authority: Statute: Department of Defense Appropriations Act, 2002, Div. B, Ch. 9, §908; 2 U.S.C. §1926. *Regulations:* None. *CFDA:* None.

Federal administering agency: U.S. Capitol Police.

Purpose of program: To recruit or retain qualified personnel.

Eligible loan type: Any student loan previously taken out by a qualifying employee (this may include FFEL and Direct Loan program Subsidized Loans, Unsubsidized Loans, PLUS Loans, and Consolidation Loans; and Perkins Loans).

Qualifying service or other activity: To qualify for repayment benefits, borrowers must be employees of the Capitol Police.

Maximum benefit amount: Up to $40,000.

Restrictions on eligibility: Repayment benefits are only available for the amount of a borrower's outstanding debts on the date a repayment agreement is executed.

Post-award conditions: N/A

Federal tax treatment: The amount of student loan repayments received is included in gross income.

Budgetary classification and funding: Discretionary. Information on previous amounts appropriated is currently unavailable to CRS.

Annual amount discharged or repaid: FY2009: $0. FY2010: $637,000. FY2011: $0. FY2012: $0. FY2013: $0.

Annual number of beneficiaries: FY2009: 0. FY2010: 103. FY2011: 0. FY2012: 0. FY2013: 0.

☐R☐ report: CRS Report RL31102, *Student Loan Repayment for Federal Employees*, by Barbara L. Schwemle and Lorraine H. Tong; archived.

Additional resources: None.

Centers for Disease Control/Agency for Toxic Substances and Disease Registry Educational Loan Repayment Program

Authority: Statute: PHSA Title III, §317F; 42 U.S.C. §247b-7. *Regulations*: None. *CFDA:* None.

Federal administering agency: Centers for Diseases Control and Prevention (CDC) and Agency for Toxic Substances and Disease Registry (ATSDR).

Purpose of program: To provide loan repayment benefits for health professionals conducting prevention activities at the CDC or the ATSDR.

Eligible loan types: Government and private loans obtained for tuition, other educational expenses, and reasonable living expenses for undergraduate education, graduate education, or both.

Qualifying service or other activity: To qualify for repayment benefits, borrowers must be CDC or ATSDR employees serving in hard-to-fill positions. Borrowers must complete at least three years of service.

Maximum benefit amount: Up to $35,000 per year.

Restrictions on eligibility: Borrowers must have a substantial amount of education loans relative to income (i.e., debt is more than 20% of a borrower's annual federal salary). Borrowers must be U.S. citizens and must hold a relevant doctoral degree or its equivalent.

Post-award conditions: Borrowers must pay an amount equal to the sum of: (1) the amount of loan repayments paid to the participant for a period of service not completed; (2) $7,500 multiplied by the months of service not completed; and (3) the interest on the sum of (1) and (2) calculated at the maximum prevailing rate—as determined by the Treasury—from the date of the contract breach if they fail to complete their service commitment.

Federal tax treatment: Borrowers can receive an additional 39% of the total loan repayment amount for federal income tax liability.

Budgetary classification and funding: Discretionary. Authorization expired in FY2002.

Annual amounts discharged or repaid: N/A

Annual number of beneficiaries: N/A

R reports: None.

Additional resources: The program was initiated as a pilot program, see Department of Health and Human Services, Centers for Disease Control and Prevention, "CDC/ATSDR Educational Loan Repayment Program," 66 *Federal Register* 54528, October 29, 2001.

Indian Health Service: Mental Health Prevention and Treatment Loan Repayment Program

Authority: Statute: Indian Health Care Improvement Act, Title I, §209(f); 25 U.S.C. §1621h. *Regulations:* None. *CFDA:* None.

Federal administering agency: U.S. Department of Health and Human Services, Indian Health Service (IHS).

Purpose of program: To recruit and retain personnel providing mental health services.

Eligible loan types: Loans used to pursue a health profession education.

Qualifying service or other activity: To qualify for repayment benefits, borrowers must be IHS employees. The duration of the service commitment is undetermined, as the program has not yet been implemented. Priority is given to borrowers who provide mental health services to children and adolescents with mental health problems.

Maximum benefit amount: Undetermined, as the program has not yet been implemented.

Restrictions on eligibility: Undetermined, as the program has not yet been implemented.

Post-award conditions: Undetermined, as the program has not yet been implemented.

Federal tax treatment: Undetermined, as the program has not yet been implemented.

Budgetary classification and funding: Discretionary. The program has not yet received any appropriations.

Annual amounts discharged or repaid: N/A

Annual number of beneficiaries: N/A

▢R▢ reports: CRS Report R41630, *The Indian Health Care Improvement Act Reauthorization and Extension as Enacted by the ACA: Detailed Summary and Timeline,* by Elayne J. Heisler; and CRS Report R43330, *The Indian Health Service (IHS): An Overview,* by Elayne J. Heisler.

Additional resources: None.

Armed Forces National Call to Service Payment of Student Loans

Authority: *Statute:* National Defense Authorization Act for Fiscal Year 2003, Div. A, Title V, Subtitle D, §531(a)(1); 10 U.S.C. §510. *Regulations:* None. *CFDA:* 64.115.

Federal administering agency: Department of Defense, applicable military branch.

Purpose of program: To serve as an incentive to individuals to enlist for active-duty service in a military occupational specialty designated as facilitating a pursuit of national service.

Eligible loan type: Any loan used to pay all or part of the cost of attendance at an institution of higher education (this may include FFEL and Direct Loan program Subsidized Loans, Unsubsidized Loans, PLUS Loans, and Consolidation Loans; Perkins Loans; and private education loans).

Qualifying service or other activity: To qualify for repayment benefits, borrowers must not have previously served in the armed forces and must enter into an original enlistment in which they agree to perform a period of national service. A period of national service includes 15 months of active duty in a military occupational specialty designated by the Secretary of Defense and either

- an additional period of active duty as determined by the Secretary of Defense; or
- 24 months of active status in the Selected Reserve.

Additionally, borrowers must then serve the remaining period of obligated service either

- on active duty in the Armed Forces;
- in the Selected Reserve;
- in AmeriCorps or another domestic national service program jointly designated by the Secretary of Defense and the head of the program for purposes of the statute; or
- in any combination of service described above.

Generally, these requirements total three years of service.

Maximum benefit amount: Up to $18,000.

Restrictions on eligibility: Benefits are only available for the amount of a borrower's outstanding student loan debt on the date that a service agreement is entered.

Post-award conditions: Borrowers must repay the amount equal to the unearned portion of the loan repayments if they fail to complete their service.

Federal tax treatment: The amount of student loan repayments received is included in gross income.

Budgetary classification and funding: Discretionary. Amounts appropriated are included as part of the relevant military service component's personnel appropriation.

nnual amount discharged or repaid: Marine Corps, FY2009: $295,000. FY2010: $15,000. FY2011: $40,000. FY2012: $0. FY2013: $0.

Information for other armed services is currently unavailable to CRS.

nnual number of beneficiaries: Information currently unavailable to CRS.

R reports: None.

dditional resources: None.

Education Loan Repayment Program: Commissioned Officers in Specified Health Professions

Authority: Statute: National Defense Authorization Act for Fiscal Year 1998, Div. A, Title VI, Subtitle E, §651(a); 10 U.S.C. §2173. *Regulations:* None. *CFDA:* None.

Federal administering agency: Department of Defense, applicable military branch.

Purpose of program: To maintain a sufficient number of active duty commissioned officers who are qualified in specified health professions.

Eligible loan type: Any loan used to finance a health profession education and used to pay for educational expenses (this may include FFEL and Direct Loan program Subsidized Loans, Unsubsidized Loans, PLUS Loans, and Consolidation Loans, Perkins Loans, and private education loans).

Qualifying service or other activity: To qualify for repayment benefits, borrowers must be fully qualified for or appointed as commissioned officers in one of the specified health professions and either be

- fully qualified healthcare professionals in an area designated by the Secretary of the relevant military department as necessary to meet a skill shortage;

- enrolled as full-time students in the final year of a course of study at an accredited institution leading to a degree in a health profession other than medicine or osteopathic medicine;

- enrolled in the final year of an approved graduate program leading to specialty qualification in medicine, dentistry, osteopathic medicine, or other health profession; or

- enrolled in the Armed Forces Health Professions Scholarship and Financial Assistance Program for a number of years less than required to complete the normal length or study.

Borrowers must serve on active duty for at least one year or, if currently on active duty, remain on active duty for an additional period of time.

Maximum benefit amount: Up to $60,000 per year. The maximum amount is increased annually by an amount equal to the percent increase in the average annual cost of educational expenses of a scholarship under the Armed Forces Health Professions Scholarship and Financial Assistance Program. The Army, Navy, and Air Force have set a maximum benefit amount at $40,000 per year of obligated service. The Army offers up to $120,000 in cumulative benefits; the Navy and Air Force offer up to the total balance of the loan.

Restrictions on eligibility: Students of the Uniformed Services University of Health Sciences cannot receive repayment benefits.

Post-award conditions: Borrowers who are commissioned officers and who are relieved of their officer's active duty obligations under the program may be given alternative obligations.

Borrowers who do not complete the active duty service or an alternative obligation must repay an amount equal to the unearned portion of student loan payments.

Federal tax treatment: The amount of student loan repayments received is included in gross income.

Budgetary classification and funding: Discretionary. Amounts appropriated are included as part of the relevant military service component's personnel appropriation.

Annual amount discharged or repaid: Information currently unavailable to CRS.

Annual number of beneficiaries: Information currently unavailable to CRS.

CR report: CRS Report RL32516, *Student Loan Forgiveness Programs*, by Gail McCallion.

Additional resources: National Council of Higher Education Loan Programs, Program Regulations Committee, "Matrix of Department of Defense (DOD) and Other Federal Student Loan Repayment Programs," February 2, 2012, http://c.ymcdn.com/sites/www.ncher.us/resource/collection/F4EAF7F5-F223-4EC9-9C0E-5511898606A6/02-08-13_DOD_Repayment_Matrix.pdf.

Armed Forces Student Loan Interest Payment Program: Members on Active Duty

Authority: Statute: National Defense Authorization Act for Fiscal Year 2003, Div. A, Title VI, Subtitle F, §651(a)(1); 10 U.S.C. §2174. *Regulations:* None. *CFDA:* None.

Federal administering agency: Department of Defense, applicable military branch.

Purpose of program: To pay for interest accrued on student loans of military personnel while they are on active duty.

Eligible loan type: Interest and special allowances that accrue on FFEL and Direct Loan program Subsidized Loans, Unsubsidized Loans, and PLUS Loans and Perkins loans.

Qualifying service or other activity: To qualify for repayment benefits, borrowers must be members of the armed forces who are on active duty in fulfillment of their first enlistment or active-duty officers who have not completed more than three years of service.

Maximum benefit allowed: Any interest and special allowances that accrue on one or more student loans to be paid for a maximum of 36 consecutive months.

Restrictions on eligibility: Loans on which interest is to be paid may not be in default.

Post-award conditions: N/A

Federal tax treatment: The amount of student loan repayments received is included in gross income.

Budgetary classification and funding: Discretionary. Amounts appropriated are included as part of the relevant military service component's personnel appropriation.

Annual amount discharged or repaid: Information currently unavailable to CRS.

Annual number of beneficiaries: Information currently unavailable to CRS.

CRS report: CRS Report RL32516, *Student Loan Forgiveness Programs*, by Gail McCallion.

Additional resources: None.

Coast Guard Education Loan Repayment Program

uthority: Statute: Coast Guard and Maritime Transportation Act of 2004, Title II, §218(a); 14 U.S.C. §472. *Regulations:* None. *CFDA:* None.

Federal administering agency: Department of Homeland Security.

Purpose of program: To recruit and retain qualified enlisted members in determined specialty occupations.

Eligible loan type: FFEL and Direct Loan program Subsidized Loans, Unsubsidized Loans, PLUS Loans, and Consolidation Loans and Perkins loans.

Qualifying service or other activity: To qualify for repayment benefits, borrowers must serve in active duty as enlisted members of the Coast Guard in a determined specialty occupation. Payment is made based upon each complete year of service performed.

Maximum benefit allowed: The greater of 33 1/3% of the outstanding student loan or $1,500 per year.

Restrictions on eligibility: N/A

Post-award conditions: N/A

Federal tax treatment: The amount of student loan repayments received is included in gross income.

Budgetary classification and funding: Discretionary. Information on previous amounts appropriated is currently unavailable to CRS.

nnual amount discharged or repaid: Information currently unavailable to CRS.

nnual beneficiaries: Information currently unavailable to CRS.

R reports: None.

dditional resources: None.

National Indian Forest Resources Management Postgraduation Recruitment Assumption of Student Loans

Authority: Statute: National Indian Forest Resource Management Act, Title III, §315; 25 U.S.C. §3114. *Regulations*: 25 C.F.R. §163.41. *CFDA:* None.

Federal administering agency: Department of the Interior, Bureau of Indian Affairs (BIA).

Purpose of program: To recruit Indian and Alaska Native graduate foresters and trained forestry technicians into the Bureau of Indian Affairs forestry programs.

Eligible loan type: Any outstanding student loan from an established lending institution (this may include FFEL and Direct Loan program Subsidized Loans, Unsubsidized Loans, PLUS Loans, and Consolidation Loans; Perkins Loans; and private education loans).

Qualifying activity or other service: To qualify for repayment benefits, borrowers must be Indian or Alaska Native professional foresters or forester technicians who have completed a post-secondary forestry or forestry-related curriculum at an accredited institution and enter into a service agreement with a BIA or tribal forestry program. Payment is made based upon each complete year of service performed.

Maximum benefit allowed: Up to $5,000 per year.

Restrictions on eligibility: N/A

Post-award conditions: Borrowers must repay the amount, plus interest, of their loans assumed by the agency if they fail to complete their service. The amount to be repaid is adjusted based on the amount of obligated service performed.

Federal tax treatment: The amount of student loan repayments received is included in gross income.

Budgetary classification and funding: Discretionary. Information on previous amounts appropriated is currently unavailable to CRS.

Annual amount discharged or repaid: Information currently unavailable to CRS.

Annual number of beneficiaries: Information currently unavailable to CRS.

CRS reports: None.

Additional Resources: None.

American Indian Agricultural Resource Management Postgraduation Recruitment Assumption of Student Loans

Authority: Statute: American Indian Agricultural Resource Management Act, Title II, §202; 25 U.S.C. §3732. *Regulations:* 25 C.F.R. §166.900 et seq. *CFDA:* None.

Federal administering agency: Department of the Interior, Bureau of Indian Affairs (BIA).

Purpose of program: To recruit Indian and Alaska Natives for employment as natural resource and trained agriculture technicians in approved agriculture programs.

Eligible loan type: Any outstanding student loan from an established lending institution (this may include FFEL and Direct Loan program Subsidized Loans, Unsubsidized Loans, PLUS Loans, and Consolidation Loans; Perkins Loans; and private education loans).

Qualifying service or other activity: To qualify for repayment benefits, borrowers must be Indian or Alaska Native natural resources and agriculture technicians who have completed a post-secondary natural resources or agriculture-related curriculum at an accredited institution and enter into a service agreement with a BIA or a tribal agriculture program or related programs. Payment is made based upon each complete year of service performed.

Maximum benefit allowed: Up to $5,000 per year.

Restrictions on eligibility: N/A

Post-award conditions: Borrowers must repay the amount, plus interest, of their loans assumed by the agency if they fail to complete their service. The amount required to be repaid is adjusted based on the amount of obligated service performed.

Federal tax treatment: The amount of student loan repayments received is included in gross income.

Budgetary classification and funding: Discretionary. Information on previous amounts appropriated is currently unavailable to CRS.

Annual amount discharged or repaid: Information currently unavailable to CRS.

Annual number of beneficiaries: Information currently unavailable to CRS.

CRS reports: None.

Additional resources: None.

Loan Repayment Program for Clinical Researchers from Disadvantaged Backgrounds

□uthority: Statute: Caregivers and Veterans Omnibus Health Services Act of 2010, Title VI, §604, P.L. 111-163; 38 U.S.C. §7681. *Regulations:* None. *CFDA:* None.

Federal administering agency: U.S. Department of Veterans Affairs, Veterans Health Administration (VHA).

Purpose of program: To recruit qualified health professionals who are from disadvantaged backgrounds to conduct clinical research for the VHA.

Eligible loan types: Loans used to pay all or part of the cost of tuition and reasonable educational and living expenses to obtain a health professional degree (this may include FFEL and Direct Loan program Subsidized Loans, Unsubsidized Loans, PLUS Loans, and Consolidation Loans; Perkins Loans; and private education loans).

*Qualifying service or other activity***:** To qualify for repayment benefits, borrowers must conduct clinical research as VHA employees and be from disadvantaged backgrounds defined by environmental or family economic circumstances.

Maximum benefit amount: Up to $35,000 per year.

Restrictions on eligibility: Borrowers must be U.S. citizens or permanent legal residents and must have obtained a health professional doctoral degree (i.e., a PhD or a doctorate in medicine, osteopathic medicine, dentistry, pharmacy, veterinary medicine, or an equivalent). Borrowers with a federal judgment or lien against their property are ineligible. Borrowers must not have received support from any of the following programs: Physicians Shortage Area Scholarship Program, National Research Service Award Program, Public Health Service Scholarship Program, National Health Service Corps Scholarship Program, Primary Care Loan Program, Armed Forces (Army, Navy, or Air Force) Professions Scholarship Program, and the Indian Health Service Scholarship Program. Borrowers who have received a deferral from one of these programs may be eligible.

Post-award conditions: Borrowers must pay $7,500 per month of service not completed, plus all the amounts paid on their behalf for the months of service that were not completed. Borrowers must also pay interest on the amount owed, with interest accruing from the date of breach. The U.S. government is entitled to recover not less than $31,000. Borrowers may terminate renewal contracts at any time without penalties. Loan repayments are prorated and terminated on the date that research stops.

Federal tax treatment: Borrowers can receive an additional 39% of the total loan repayment amount for income tax liability.

Budgetary classification and funding: Discretionary. This program is part of the VA's Education Debt Reduction Program, and funding for this program is included as part of amounts appropriated for that program. FY2009: $13.7 million. FY2010: $17 million. FY2011: $17.3 million. FY2012: $19.2 million. FY2013 (estimated): $18.0 million.

nnual amounts discharged or repaid: Information currently unavailable to CRS.

nnual number of beneficiaries: Information currently unavailable to CRS.

R reports: None.

dditional resources: None.

Appendix B. Programs by Eligibility

Tables B-2 through B-5 list federal student loan repayment and forgiveness programs by type of profession or service that qualifies borrowers for program benefits. Table B-6 lists federal student loan repayment and forgiveness programs that are based, in part, on a borrower's financial circumstances. Within each table, programs are organized according to their order of presentation in the report (i.e., in descending order intended to be reflective of potential scale of availability to borrowers and financial resources needed to provide benefits). The following tables list a brief description of the eligibility criteria, length of service commitment, qualifying loan type, maximum benefit available, and administering agency or entity. For more complete information on each program, see the program-specific details listed in □□□□□□□□. Programs with columns denoted "undetermined" have not yet been implemented and, therefore, may have some criteria that have not yet been established. Finally, several programs (e.g., the Public Service Loan Forgiveness Program) benefit a variety of professions and, therefore, may appear in multiple tables.

□□□□□□□□identifies the meanings of acronyms used in the tables that follow.

Table B-1. Acronyms used in Table B-2 through Table B-6

ATSDR	Agency for Toxic Substances and Disease Registry
BIA	Bureau of Indian Affairs
BJA	Bureau of Justice Assistance
CDC	Centers for Disease Control and Prevention
CBO	Congressional Budget Office
CNCS	Corporation for National and Community Service
DL	William D. Ford Federal Direct Loan program
DHS	Department of Homeland Security
DOD	Department of Defense
DOI	Department of the Interior
DOJ	Department of Justice
DOS	Department of State
ED	Department of Education
FDA	Food and Drug Administration
FFEL	Federal Family Education Loan program
HHS	Department of Health and Human Services
HPSA	Health Professional Shortage Areas
IHS	Indian Health Service
JRJ	John R. Justice
LRP	Loan Repayment Program
NCCC	National Civilian Community Corps
NHSC	National Health Service Corps
NIFA	National Institute of Food and Agriculture

NIH	National Institutes of Health
PHSA	Public Health Service Act
STEM	Science, Technology, Engineering, and Mathematics
USCG	U.S. Coast Guard
USDA	U.S. Department of Agriculture
VA	U.S. Department of Veterans Affairs
VHA	Veterans Health Administration
VISTA	Volunteers in Service to America

Table B-2. Federal Student Loan Repayment and Forgiveness Programs

Healthcare and Public Health Professions

Program	Administering Agency/Entity	Eligibility	Service Commitment	Qualifying Loans	Maximum Benefit
DL Public Service Loan Forgiveness	ED	Employed full-time in a public health services organization	10 years	DL program Subsidized Loans, Unsubsidized Loans, PLUS Loans, and Consolidation Loans	Remaining loan balance after 10 years of qualifying payments
Federal Perkins Loan Cancellation	ED	Employed full-time as a nurse or medical technician	At least 1 year for partial benefit; 5 years for maximum benefit	Federal Perkins Loans	100% of student loan balance
IHS Loan Repayment Program	HHS/IHS	Health professionals employed at an IHS facility in a specifically identified field	At least 2 years	Loans used to finance educational expenses	$35,000 per year
NHSC LRP	HHS/HRSA	Health professionals in health professional shortage areas, including clinical social workers, family therapists, and counselors	At least 2 years	Loans used to finance educational expenses	$60,000 per year; $240,000 in total
NHSC Students to Service LRP	HHS/HRSA	Primary care health professionals in health professional shortage areas of greatest need	At least 3 years	Loans used to finance educational expenses	$60,000 per year; $120,000 in total
National Health Service Corps State LRP	HHS/HRSA	Health professionals in state-designated shortage areas	Varies by state	Loans used to finance educational expenses	Varies by state
NIH Extramural LRP: Health Disparities Research	HHS/NIH	Health professionals who conduct health disparities research at an eligible institution	At least 2 years	FFEL, DL, PLUS, and Consolidation loans, PHSA Title VII-A and VIII-B loans, and loans made by certain government and private lenders	$35,000 per year

CRS-126

Program	Administering Agency/Entity	Eligibility	Service Commitment	Qualifying Loans	Maximum Benefit
NIH Extramural LRP: Contraception and Infertility Research	HHS/NIH	Health professionals who conduct contraception and/or fertility research at an eligible institution	At least 2 years	FFEL, DL, PLUS, and Consolidation loans, PHSA Title VII-A and VIII-B loans, and loans made by certain government and private lenders	$35,000 per year
NIH Extramural LRP: Clinical Research	HHS/NIH	Health professionals who conduct clinical research at eligible institutions	At least 2 years	FFEL, DL, PLUS, and Consolidation loans, PHSA Title VII-A and VIII-B loans, and loans made by certain government and private lenders	$35,000 per year
NIH Extramural LRP: Pediatric Research	HHS/NIH	Health professionals who conduct pediatric research at eligible institutions	At least 2 years	FFEL, DL, PLUS, and Consolidation loans, PHSA Title VII-A and VIII-B loans, loans made by certain government and private lenders	$35,000 per year
Loan Repayments for Health Professional School Faculty	HHS/HRSA	Health professionals who agree to serve as faculty at a health professions school	At least 2 years	Loans used to finance educational expenses	$40,000 per year
General, Pediatric, and Public Health Dentistry Faculty Loan Payment	HHS/HRSA	Full-time faculty in general, pediatric, or public health dentistry	5 years	Undetermined	100% of student loan balance
Nursing Education LRP (NURSE Corps)	HHS/HRSA	Nurses at nonprofit healthcare facilities with a shortage of nurses or nurse faculty members at accredited nursing schools	At least 2 years	Loans used to finance educational expenses	85% of student loan balance
Nursing Faculty LRP	HHS/HRSA	Full-time nurse faculty at accredited nursing schools	At least 1 year	Loans used to finance educational expenses	85% of student loan balance, plus interest

Program	Administering Agency/Entity	Eligibility	Service Commitment	Qualifying Loans	Maximum Benefit
Public Health Workforce LRP	HHS/HRSA	Full-time public health professionals	At least 3 years	Loans used to finance educational expenses	$35,000 per year
Loan Forgiveness for Service in Areas of National Need	ED	Employed as a nurse, public or mental health professional, or dentist	None	FFEL and DL program Subsidized Loans, Unsubsidized Loans, Graduate PLUS Loans, and Consolidation Loans (other than those used to repay Parent PLUS Loans)	$2,000 per year; $10,000 in total
Pediatric Subspecialist LRP	HHS/HRSA	Full-time pediatric health professionals who are employed in a HPSA or underserved area	At least 2 years	Loans used to finance educational expenses	$35,000 per year
Nursing Workforce Development Loans: Loan Cancellation	HHS/HRSA	Professional full-time nurses at eligible institutions; loans must have been received before September 29, 1995	Undetermined	Loans made to students by schools from funds established under the program's statute	85% of student loan balance
Nursing Workforce Development Student Loans: Loan Repayment	HHS/HRSA	Borrower is unable to complete nursing studies, is in exceptionally needy circumstances, and does not resume studies within two years of withdrawal from studies	Undetermined	Loans made to students by schools from funds established under the program's statute	Undetermined
Eligible Individual Student LRP	HHS/HRSA	Licensed nurses with a master's or doctoral degree who serve as full-time nursing faculty	At least 4 years	Undetermined	$20,000 per year; $80,000 in total

Program	Administering Agency/Entity	Eligibility	Service Commitment	Qualifying Loans	Maximum Benefit
LRP: Health Professions Officers Serving in the Selected Reserve with Wartime Critical Medical Skill Shortages	DOD	Officers in the Selected Reserve who are qualified, or enrolled in a program leading to qualification, in a critically needed healthcare profession to meet wartime combat medical shortages	At least 1 year	FFEL and DL program Subsidized Loans, Unsubsidized Loans, Graduate PLUS Loans, and Consolidation Loans, Perkins Loans, PHSA Title VII-A and VIII-B loans, Primary Care Loan Program loans, and private education loans	$60,000 per year
Federal Food, Drug, and Cosmetic Act LRP	HHS/FDA	Health professionals who conduct research as an FDA employee and whose debt exceeds 20% of their annual salary	At least 3 years	Loans used to finance educational expenses	$20,000 per year
Education Debt Reduction Program	VA/VHA	VHA health professionals who provide direct patient care in specified fields, including social work and speech pathology	None	Loans used to finance educational expenses	$60,000 in total over a five year period
NIH Intramural LRP: AIDS Research	HHS/NIH	NIH employees who conduct clinical AIDS research	At least 2 years	FFEL, DL, PLUS, and Consolidation loans, PHSA Title VII-A and VIII-B loans, and loans made by certain government and private lenders	$35,000 per year
NIH Intramural LRP: General Research	HHS/NIH	NIH employees who conduct research	At least 3 years	FFEL, DL, PLUS, and Consolidation loans, PHSA Title VII-A and VIII-B loans, and loans made by certain government and private lenders	$35,000 per year

Program	Administering Agency/Entity	Eligibility	Service Commitment	Qualifying Loans	Maximum Benefit
NIH Intramural LRP: General Research for Accreditation Council for Graduate Medical Education Fellows	HHS/NIH	NIH Accreditation Council for Graduate Medical Education fellows	At least 3 years of service	FFEL, DL, PLUS, and Consolidation loans, PHSA Title VII-A and VIII-B loans, and loans made by certain government and private lenders	$17,000 per year
NIH Intramural LRP: Clinical Researchers from Disadvantaged Backgrounds	HHS/NIH	NIH employees from disadvantaged backgrounds who conduct clinical research	At least 2 years of service	FFEL, DL, PLUS, and Consolidation loans, PHSA Title VII-A and VIII-B loans, and loans made by certain government and private lenders	$35,000 per year
CDC/ATSDR Educational LRP	HHS /CDC/ATSDR	CDC or ATSDR employees in hard-to-fill positions and whose debt exceeds 20% of their salary	At least 3 years	Loans used to finance educational expenses	$35,000 per year
IHS Mental Health Prevention and Treatment LRP	HHS/IHS	IHS employees who provide mental health services	Undetermined	Loans used to finance educational expenses	Undetermined
LRP: Commissioned Officers in Specified Health Professions	DOD	Members who are serving or able to serve on active duty as an officer in a specified healthcare profession	At least 1 year	Loans used to finance a health profession education	$60,000 per year
LRP: Clinical Researchers from Disadvantaged Backgrounds	VA/VHA	VHA employees from disadvantaged backgrounds who conduct clinical research	At least 1 year	Loans used to finance educational expenses	$35,000 per year

Source: CRS analysis of relevant statutes, regulations, and program materials.

Table B-3. Federal Student Loan Repayment and Forgiveness Programs

Education Professions

Program	Administering Agency/Entity	Eligibility	Service Commitment	Qualifying Loans	Maximum Benefit
DL Public Service Loan Forgiveness	ED	Employed full-time in a public education or public library services organization	10 years	DL program Subsidized Loans, Unsubsidized Loans, PLUS Loans, and Consolidation Loans	Remaining loan balance after 10 years of qualifying payments
Stafford Loan Forgiveness for Teachers	ED	Full-time teachers in public or private nonprofit schools or public education service agencies	At least 5 consecutive complete academic years	FFEL and DL program Subsidized Loans and Unsubsidized Loans; and portions of Consolidation Loans attributable to Subsidized Loans and Unsubsidized Loans	$5,000 in general; $17,500 for special education and STEM teachers
Federal Perkins Loan Cancellation	ED	Employed full-time in specified education services	At least 1 year for partial benefit; 5 years for maximum benefit	Federal Perkins Loans	100% of student loan balance
Loan Repayments for Health Professional School Faculty	HHS/HRSA	Health professionals who agree to serve as faculty at a health professions school	At least 2 years	Loans used to finance educational expenses	$40,000 per year
General, Pediatric, and Public Health Dentistry Faculty Loan Payment	HHS/HRSA	Full-time faculty in general, pediatric, or public health dentistry	5 years	Undetermined	100% of student loan balance
Nursing Education LRP (NURSE Corps)	HHS/HRSA	Nurse faculty members at accredited nursing schools	At least 2 years	Loans used to finance educational expenses	85% of student loan balance
Nursing Faculty LRP	HHS/HRSA	Full-time nurse faculty at accredited nursing schools	At least 1 year	Loans used to finance educational expenses	85% of student loan balance, plus interest

Program	Administering Agency/Entity	Eligibility	Service Commitment	Qualifying Loans	Maximum Benefit
Loan Forgiveness for Service in Areas of National Need	ED	Full-time teachers, librarians, school counselors, and school administrators	At least 1 year	FFEL and DL program Subsidized Loans, Unsubsidized Loans, Graduate PLUS, and Consolidation Loans (other than those used to repay Parent PLUS Loans)	$2,000 per year; $10,000 in total
Nursing Workforce Development Loans: Loan Cancellation	HHS/HRSA	Professional full-time nursing teachers at eligible institutions; loans must have been received before September 29, 1995	Undetermined	Loans made to students by schools from funds established under the program's statute	85% of student loan balance
Eligible Individual Student LRP	HHS/HRSA	Licensed nurses with a master's or doctoral degree who serve as full-time nursing faculty	At least 4 years	Undetermined	$20,000 per year; $80,000 in total

Source: CRS analysis of relevant statutes, regulations, and program materials.

Table B-4. Federal Student Loan Repayment and Forgiveness Programs

Public Service Professions (Other than Healthcare, Education, and Military)

Program	Administering Agency/Entity	Eligibility	Service Commitment	Qualifying Loans	Maximum Benefit
DL Public Service Loan Forgiveness Program	ED	Employed full-time in a public organization providing emergency management, public safety, public interest law, elderly, or disability services	10 years	DL program Subsidized Loans, Unsubsidized Loans, PLUS Loans, and Consolidation Loans	Remaining loan balance after 10 years of qualifying payments
Federal Perkins Loan Cancellation	ED	Employed full-time in specified public service professions, including Peace Corps and AmeriCorps VISTA	At least 1 year for partial benefit; 5 years for maximum benefit	Federal Perkins Loans	100% of student loan balance
Veterinary Medicine LRP	USDA/NIFA	Large animal veterinarians who provide short-term emergency services to the federal government	60 days of service per year for at least 3 years	Loans used to finance educational expenses	$25,000 per year
JRJ Loan Repayment for Prosecutors and Public Defenders Program	DOJ/BJA	Full-time prosecutors, public defenders, and federal defenders	At least 3 years	FFEL, DL, Graduate PLUS, Consolidation, and Perkins loans	$10,000 per year; $60,000 in total
Civil Legal Assistance Attorney Student LRP	ED	Full-time civil legal assistance attorneys	At least 3 years	FFEL and DL program Subsidized Loans, Unsubsidized Loans, Graduate PLUS, and Consolidation Loans (other than those used to repay Parent PLUS Loans) and Perkins Loans	$6,000 per year; $40,000 in total

Program	Administering Agency/Entity	Eligibility	Service Commitment	Qualifying Loans	Maximum Benefit
Loan Forgiveness for Service in Areas of National Need	ED	Full-time public safety, emergency management, public interest legal services, or STEM professionals	At least 1 year	FFEL and DL program Subsidized Loans, Unsubsidized Loans, Graduate PLUS, and Consolidation Loans (other than those used to repay Parent PLUS Loans)	$2,000 per year; $10,000 in total
LRP for Senate Employees	Secretary of the Senate	Senate or Office of Congressional Accessibility Services employees	At least 1 year	FFEL, DL, PLUS, Consolidation, and Perkins loans, PHSA Title VII-A and VIII-E loans	$500 per month; $40,000 in total
LRP for House Employees	Committee on House Administration	U.S. House of Representatives employees	At least 1 year	FFEL, DL, PLUS, Consolidation, and Perkins loans, PHSA Title VII-A and VIII-E loans	$833 per month; $60,000 in total
CBO Student Loan Repayment	CBO	CBO employees	At least 1 year	Loans used to finance educational expenses	$6,000 per year; $40,000 in total
Government Employee LRP	Individual Executive Agencies	Federal executive branch agency employees and certain legislative branch agency employees	At least 3 years	FFEL, DL, PLUS, Consolidation, and Perkins loans, PHSA Title VII-A and VIII-E loans	$10,000 per year; $60,000 in total
Defense Acquisition Workforce LRP	DOD	DOD civilian acquisition personnel	At least 3 years	FFEL, DL, PLUS, Consolidation, and Perkins loans, PHSA Title VII-A and VIII-E loans	$10,000 per year; $60,000 in total
National and Community Service Grant program, Educational Award	CNCS	Individuals who complete service in AmeriCorps, NCCC, or VISTA	Completion of service in AmeriCorps, NCCC, or VISTA	FFEL, DL, PLUS, Consolidation, and Perkins loans, PHSA title VII-A and VIII-E loans, and other loans determined necessary to finance educational expenses	Equal to the maximum Pell Grant award in effect at the beginning of the year in which the CNCS approves the individual's service position

Program	Administering Agency/Entity	Eligibility	Service Commitment	Qualifying Loans	Maximum Benefit
Capitol Police LRP	Capitol Police	Capitol Police employees	N/A	Loans used to finance educational expenses	$40,000 in total
National Indian Forest Resources Management Postgraduation Recruitment Assumption of Student Loans	DOI/BIA	Indians or Alaska Natives who serve as professional foresters or forester technicians for the BIA or a tribal forestry program	At least 1 year	Loans used to finance educational expenses	$5,000 per year
American Indian Agricultural Resource Management Postgraduation Recruitment Assumption of Loans	DOI/BIA	Indians or Alaska Natives who serve as professional natural resources and agriculture technicians for the BIA or tribal agriculture program	At least 1 year	Loans used to finance educational expenses	$5,000 per year

Source: CRS analysis of relevant statutes, regulations, and program materials.

Table B-5. Federal Student Loan Repayment and Forgiveness Programs

Military Service

Program	Administering Agency/Entity	Eligibility	Service Commitment	Qualifying Loans	Maximum Benefit
DL Public Service Loan Forgiveness Program	ED	Employed full-time in a public organization	10 years	DL program Subsidized Loans, Unsubsidized Loans, PLUS Loans, and Consolidation Loans	Remaining loan balance after 10 years of qualifying payments
LRP: Enlisted Members on Active Duty in Specified Military Specialties	DOD	Members who perform active duty in certain officer programs or military specialties	At least 1 year	FFEL, DL, PLUS, Consolidation, and Perkins loans, state and private education loans	The greater of 33 1/3% of the outstanding loan or $1,500 per year
LRP: Members of the Selected Reserve	DOD	Members of the Selected Reserve in certain officer programs or enlisted military specialties	At least 1 year	FFEL, DL, PLUS, Consolidation, and Perkins loans, state and private education loans	The greater of 15% of the outstanding loan or $500 per year, plus accrued interest
LRP: Health Professions Officers Serving in Selected Reserve with Wartime Critical Medical Skill Shortages	DOD	Officers in the Selected Reserve who are qualified, or enrolled in a program leading to qualification, in a critically needed healthcare profession to meet wartime combat medical shortages	At least one year	FFEL, DL, Graduate PLUS and Perkins loans, PHSA Title VII-A and VII-B loans, Primary Care Loan Program loans, and private education loans	$60,000/year
LRP: Chaplains Serving in the Selected Reserve	DOD	Members serving or able to serve as a chaplain in the Selected Reserve	At least 3 years	Loans used to finance educational expenses	$20,000 per three years
Armed Forces National Call to Service	DOD	Members who enlist and serve in a designated military occupational specialty	At least 15 months of active duty, plus additional active or reserve service	Loans used to finance educational expenses	$18,000 in total

Program	Administering Agency/Entity	Eligibility	Service Commitment	Qualifying Loans	Maximum Benefit
LRP: Commissioned Officers in Specified Health Professions	DOD	Members who are serving or able to serve on active duty as an officer in a specified healthcare profession	At least 1 year	Loans used to finance a health profession education	$60,000 per year
Armed Forces Student Loan Interest Payment Program: Members on Active Duty	DOD	Active duty members of the armed forces in their first term of service	None	Interest and special allowances that accrue on FFEL, DL, PLUS, and Perkins loans	36 consecutive months of interest and special allowances
Coast Guard Education LRP	DHS/USCG	Enlisted members of the Coast Guard on active duty in specified occupations	At least 1 year	FFEL, DL, PLUS, Consolidation, and Perkins loans	The greater of 33 1/3% of the loan or $1,500 per year

Source: CRS analysis of relevant statutes, regulations, and program materials.

Table B-6. Federal Student Loan Repayment and Forgiveness Programs

Borrower's Financial Circumstances

Program	Administering Agency/Entity	Eligibility	Service Commitment	Qualifying Loans	Maximum Benefit
DL Public Service Loan Forgiveness Program	ED	Employed full-time in a public organization	10 years	DL program Subsidized Loans, Unsubsidized Loans, PLUS Loans, and Consolidation Loans	Remaining loan balance after 10 years of qualifying payments
Income-Contingent Repayment Plan A (or Pay As You Earn)	ED	Borrowers who make the equivalent of 20 years of payments under ICR-A or other qualifying plans; monthly payments are capped at 10% of borrower's discretionary income	N/A	DL program Subsidized Loans, Unsubsidized Loans, Graduate PLUS, and Consolidation Loans (other than those used to repay Parent PLUS Loans)	Remaining loan balance after 20 years of qualifying payments

Program	Administering Agency/Entity	Eligibility	Service Commitment	Qualifying Loans	Maximum Benefit
Income-Based Repayment Plan for New Borrowers on or after July 1, 2014	ED	Borrowers who make the equivalent of 20 years of payments under IBR or other qualifying plans ; monthly payments are capped at 10% of the borrower's discretionary income	None	DL program Subsidized Loans, Unsubsidized Loans, Graduate PLUS, and Consolidation Loans (other than those used to repay Parent PLUS Loans)	Remaining loan balance after 20 years of qualifying payments
Income-Based Repayment Plan for pre-July 1, 2014 Borrowers	ED	Borrowers who make the equivalent of 25 years of payments under IBR or other qualifying plans ;; monthly payments are capped at 15% of the borrower's discretionary income	N/A	FFEL and DL program Subsidized Loans, Unsubsidized Loans, Graduate PLUS, and Consolidation Loans (other than those used to repay Parent PLUS Loans)	Remaining loan balance after 25 years of qualifying payments
Income-Contingent Repayment Plan B	ED	Borrowers who make the equivalent of 25 years of payments under ICR-B or other qualifying plans; monthly payments are generally capped at 20% of borrower's discretionary income	N/A	DL program Subsidized Loans, Unsubsidized Loans, Graduate PLUS, and Consolidation Loans	Remaining loan balance after 25 years of qualifying payments
Nursing Workforce Development Student Loans: Loan Repayment	HHS/HRSA	Borrower is unable to complete nursing studies, is in exceptionally needy circumstances, and does not resume studies within two years of withdrawal from studies	Undetermined	Loans made to students by schools from funds established under the program's statute	Undetermined

Program	Administering Agency/Entity	Eligibility	Service Commitment	Qualifying Loans	Maximum Benefit
Federal Food, Drug, and Cosmetic Act LRP	HHS/FDA	Health professionals who conduct research as an FDA employee and whose debt exceeds 20% of their annual salary	At least 3 years	Loans used to finance educational expenses	$20,000 per year
NIH Intramural LRP: Clinical Researchers from Disadvantaged Backgrounds	HHS/NIH	NIH employees from disadvantaged backgrounds who conduct clinical research	At least 2 years of service	FFEL, DL, PLUS, and Consolidation loans, PHSA Title VII-A and VIII-B loans, loans made by certain government and private lenders	$35,000 per year
CDC/ATSDR Educational LRP	CDC/ATSDR	CDC or ATSDR employees in hard-to-fill positions and whose debt exceeds 20% of their salary	At least 3 years	Loans used to finance educational expenses	$35,000 per year
LRP: Clinical Researchers from Disadvantaged Backgrounds	VA/VHA	VHA employees from disadvantaged backgrounds who conduct clinical research	At least 1 year	FFEL, DL, PLUS, and Perkins loans	$35,000 per year

Source: CRS analysis of relevant statutes, regulations, and program materials.

Author Contact Information

Alexandra Hegji, Coordinator
Analyst in Social Policy
adhegji@crs.loc.gov , 7-8384

Elayne J. Heisler
Analyst in Health Services
eheisler@crs.loc.gov, 7-4453

David P. Smole
Specialist in Education Policy
dsmole@crs.loc.gov, 7-0624

Acknowledgements

Brittany Maschal contributed to the initial drafting of this report during an internship with the Congressional Research Service.